MW00873531

GIRLS GOT ISSUES

A Woman's Guide to
Self-discovery and Healing

Lee,

Peace! Blessings

Dr. Tyffani Monford Dent

Copyright © 2011 Dr. Tyffani Monford Dent
All rights reserved.

ISBN: 1456528122
ISBN-13: 9781456528126

ACKNOWLEDGMENTS

This has been a long process, and I must first thank the girls from the Independent Living Program who made me begin to really think about the "issues" we all face. Your resiliency in the face of extreme adversity should be admired by all

To the Women of Wilberforce University (my alma mater) who permitted me to speak at several of your Women's Summit—many talks which contributed to chapters of this book

My parents—Bobby and Mary Monford who have never attempted to live vicariously through me—but instead encouraged me to pursue my own path

My editor, Patricia Selden-Black—your "take-no-prisoners" feedback made this a better book

My best friends—Lachelle & Sunta for always being my "sister-friends"

My sorors of Delta Sigma Theta Sorority, Inc., especially Beta Chapter—you remind me why "I am my sister's keeper." The line of Spring 1995 (Nicole, Deila, Satira, Shane, Talina, Antoinette, Temeca, Davisha, Rashana, Amanda, & Kadeana)—all of you have been a part of my life's journey since that time

S. Pierre Story and Darlene Lee who seemed to labor with me by reading every draft of this book. Your criticisms, praises, and insight were valuable contributions to this book

Katia L. Wilson—-what can I say, but "what you say?" (smile)

Renee Jackson-Bradford for providing an inspirational foreword to this book and who continues to inspire me and all who come in to contact with her

Dena Patrice who contributed a wonderful section to this book. You have shared your wisdom with me and I am honored that you are sharing it in this book

Phil Rich, Michael Hagan, and David Prescott who encouraged me to write about something about which I am passionate

The "sisters" at Cleveland Christian Home-Lorain Avenue (Tonya, Darlene, Cathy, Kathy, Sylvonne, Bonnie, Susan, and many others) for their ongoing support and their free babysitting services

Kevin for an awesome book cover

Jasmine Finnie from Ohio Domestic Violence Network (ODVN) for her critique and input on the chapter on Toxic Relationships

Kirsti Mouncey from Cleveland Rape Crisis Center for her advice on "Cleaning Out Your Closet"

Amy Lane, my high school English teacher, who first introduced me to the power of words

My brothers and sisters—Bruce, Antonio, Dale, Tyrone, Kimber, Lisa, Angee, Lish, Tesa & Quantella,—just because

A special acknowledgment to Lamont and Travis—my brothers who made the Project 2010 pact with me—it was because of your encouragement that I made this book happen—even if it is a little late. Travis—you did it. Lamont, you are up next…..

The next generation of Monford women—Candis, Latrinda, Ciera, Chassidy, Mary Alice, Andrea, Brianna, Brandi, Tylar, and Rylee—may you have less "issues" to face

My sister-in-law Katina Douglas (Heartsongs Photography) for her work on my author photograph

Nette, Moira, Marsha, Terralyn, & Evelyn-mis amigas por vida

Robin Palmer—just for being you

My own babies—Mia & Zoe who, although they did not understand, still allowed mommy time to write

Lastly, to my husband Travis—who allowed me to be selfish, and loves me…in spite of my closet

DEDICATION

Because of Ladonna,
For Aunt Cheryl
&
In Honor of Sonya Lynn: who *knew*,
but never got the chance to see

TABLE OF CONTENTS

FOREWORD

Dear Friends:

My daughter inspires me. She radiates with such joy as she lavishly loves others and navigates her World. In her, I see the purest imaginings of a world that loves back. Most days I want to dream butterfly dreams with her but I am interrupted by all my "stuff". Although I am living an inspired life, I still remember. It's hard to forget the…

… head bobbin'…eye-rollin…neck turnin'…finger pointin'…loud talkin'…boyfriend stealin'…clothes rippin'…hair pullin'…"stuff".

Thank God for the moments in our lives that move us beyond ourselves to want to do better. For me, it has been my daughter. Our Mother/Daughter relationship has brought great healing to my life. I aspire to greater love with her. I refuse to translate those hurtful, unimaginable, life-exchanges that I have had with other girls into our future. Together, we are creating richer, deeper life experiences of laughter and learning. She helps me to be a better woman.

Raising Our Daughters

We are the best line of defense in preventing our daughters from becoming assailants on other girls. By facing our issues as women, we are making a proclamation in our freedom to make choices. It's our refusal to transfer useless, learned behaviors and to commit to being active participants in protecting our daughter's futures. When we choose to model drama-free, whole-selves we are promoting healthy relationships that have the potential to positively impact our communities and change our World.

Uplifting Ourselves

Girls Got Issues: A Woman's Guide to Self-Discovery and Healing is a useful tool for every woman's self-defining moments. It's our arsenal in ridding our souls of the "girl-stuff". The practical life applications of

- affirming other women,
- healing of self,
- and life introspection

found in this book are the first steps in ending the generational cycles of broken female relationships in your life. If you cannot find it within you to do it for yourself, I encourage you to do it for our daughters.

I pray that *Girls Got Issues: A Woman's Guide to Self-Discovery and Healing* will launch you forward into being all that God imagined you to be to yourself, to those you love, and to our World.

Inspired,

Rev. Renee L. Bradford, M.Div.
Founder/Vision Keeper
First Purse, Inc.

INTRODUCTION

Having worked in a variety of settings with adolescents and adults, one of the things I have noticed when I tell others that I am doing work with girls/women is the change in their expressions. They lean back, frown, and often shake their heads before announcing to me that, "Girls got issues." I would find myself defending my, admittedly part-time, work with girls and discussing the resilience of those with whom I worked. However, when I discovered that I was having my first daughter and then a second one a few years later I, too, shook my head and worried if my girls would "have issues." Oftentimes, we, as women, are worse on our gender than men could possibly be towards us. Yet, I admit openly now that "Girls got issues"— but also that we must look closely to determine from where our issues originate. We must also begin to face these "issues" head on, so that we do not take them in to adulthood and they become "Women Problems."

True, there are some "issues" that are beyond our control, such as the fact that 1 in 6 of us will be sexually abused in our lifetime.[1] In addition, we, as women, are more likely to be battered by our partners than our male counterparts[2]. Even the fact that we are often smaller in size and physically not as strong as men presents issues that are difficult to overcome. Yet, there are things that are within our control—that we have for some reason chosen to embrace as "just being a part of being female" instead of examining within

---

[1] www.rainn.org downloaded 4/3/10

[2] Bureau of Justice Statistics Crime Data Brief, *Intimate Partner Violence, 1993-2001*, February 2003.

ourselves and society what makes us more susceptible to "issues" or less willing to challenge or change them.

It is hoped that, this book will allow us to begin examining our girlhood issues that have become our womanhood problems. However, just like in any process of self-examination, we must be open to acknowledging that problems exist, become ready to tackle them and make actual change, and then actively work to do something different. Yet, in any major undertaking, we must be able to have others who join us on the journey and are there to support us. So, my sisters, I am ready to take this trip of self-discovery and healing with you. Brace yourself, the ride may be unpleasant at times, but the destination will be worth it.

Change is Good

I remember when Barack Obama began campaigning for the presidency, trumpeting the concept of "Change We Can Believe In." I would be on the street and hear people talk about Barack Obama and how he was going to bring about change. I did not marvel at people being excited by Barack Obama, but I was surprised at how the word "change" was suddenly a positive thing. For women, when people say the word "change" it often has a negative connotation, such as "Girl, you've changed," usually said with a sigh, rolling of the eye, or an accusatory finger wave. Yet, now in the Age of Barack, we are allowed to say we have changed, and have it viewed as a good thing.

We go through many stages of change. In kindergarten, someone picked out our clothes, got us up in the morning and determined every aspect of our day. Moving on to junior high, we tried to assert ourselves. We would push to have our say in decisions being made about our lives, often resulting in battles with our parents that we knew we could never win. Yet, we fought anyway, trying to get permission to begin turning into the women we wanted to become.

High school was not only about being in a new school, but having new friendships and new interests. We may have begun to drift away from those with whom we thought we would be friends with forever as we began preparing for different life paths—college or work. But change was inevitable. So what is the difficulty in embracing it? If one chooses to go off to college or go off to begin a career, that in and of itself, means change—change in finances, location, and things as basic as how your day will go. Yet, we struggle to acknowledge that these life-altering situations do not change us. Instead, we want to insist that we are the exact same person as we were before college, before careers, even before motherhood. What makes us protest and deny that we are becoming different people?

We happily embrace changes in hairstyles, clothes, etc—-both of which are superficial changes that do not require much energy or thought. However, when we are experiencing changes in our attitudes or our outlook on life, we push it away and seem to be embarrassed by it. As women, we must begin to examine where our belief that "changing is disgraceful" originated. Why do we fear it, deny it, and run from it?

Perhaps, it is due in part to the fact that those with whom we surround ourselves are not willing to make necessary changes in their lives. Is it because we are becoming the people we were destined to be, and those around us are not making that same leap—so therefore, they choose instead to denigrate our change?

It is time that we began to look at change as synonymous with evolution. In doing so, its meaning may change as well. As women, we not only grow from girlhood to womanhood, but we must allow ourselves to evolve in other ways. When we look at evolution we can define it as:

- any process of formation or growth; development
- a process of gradual, peaceful, progressive change or development

Clearly, in either definition, is the concept of a slow process in which change must occur. The ultimate goal in evolution/change is that what is occurring will result in some metamorphosis of something better.

Ameenah is a 35 year old African-American woman who had always been spiritual. In her college years, she studied various religions, knowing that she was seeking something. Reared in a Baptist home, her decision to explore other faiths was not taken as a positive sign by those in her family—even though they did not attend church regularly. Shortly after graduating from college, Ameenah discovered Islam. Converting to the faith, she then married a Muslim man and is in the process of rearing their children to be pious Muslims. Ameenah regards her change in religion as a journey that has been the best decision she ever made.

Janice is a 40-something woman who graduated from college on time and entered the world of finance. She had the car, the money, and all the other trappings that college grads wish for. Yet, within two years of being in the business world, she decided that her true calling was in social services. She decided to quit her high-powered job and work at a local non-profit agency. After 5 years of being in the non-profit arena, she decided to combine her love of finance with her desire to "give back". Janice left the non-profit agency and started her own non-profit in which she teaches fiscal responsibility and self-esteem to young girls.

Change can be difficult. Often there are major barriers to the change process. For Ameenah, it was dealing with family members who had preconceived notions about what it meant to be Muslim; as well as American society that viewed Islam as something foreign and outside of the norm. However, Ameenah overcame these barriers because she viewed Islam as an answer to her religious questions and has now surrounded herself with those who understand her decision and support her in it. For Janice, it was leaving behind financial security in order to pursue her passion and then being willing to leave even the security of full-time employment to start her own business.

Ameenah and Janice are not the first people who have contemplated changing his/her faith or career, yet many who contemplate never move forward with it. Why, if we know that change can be for the better, do we refuse to take the steps forward?

Reasons we don't change:
- *Often stressful*-Making the decision to do something different can cause us to second-guess ourselves. In addition, if those around us are content with the person that we are, they may discourage the change. We must remember that short-term stress associated with change will give away to our being true to ourselves and more content.

- *Often difficult*-I am right-handed. I don't know if I was born that way or if it was something that I learned. At one point, I had carpal tunnel, resulting in my wrist being bandaged. Figuring that I would give my right hand a break, I attempted to do more with my left hand. Quickly, I discovered that it is not that easy. I would naturally find myself reaching for things with my right or attempting to hold the telephone with it. When we do something new, we often go back to the old because it is familiar and comfortable—even if it is not in our best interest at the time. Be aware that as you begin the change process, you are likely to "backslide" into the familiar because change can be hard. The goal is to remind yourself why change is needed and work to get back on track.

- *Often not wanted by those invested in keeping you the same*-How many of you have heard "she's changed" or "she thinks she's better" when you have decided to do something different or engage in self-improvement? Often, we view people around us as a mirror into what we should be. If you are moving toward being a better you, and those around you have given themselves excuses for not changing, your willingness to "step it up" may read as not permitting them to continue to make excuses for not undertaking their own needed evolution. People around us sometimes are comfortable in their stagnation—and your unwillingness to settle makes them uncomfortable in that you then give a picture of what it is like to achieve your goals/dreams/change.

Change does not occur overnight; instead it is a process that we must go through. Just like any process, it is not an easy one, as it involves work. Being that it is work that many discourage us from engaging in, it can also be easier to not go through the process and maintain the status quo. When going through the change process, we must begin by taking a self-inventory. In counseling circles, this is often looked at through the *Stages of Change*. We need to recognize where we are in our willingness to "do something different". Are we at *pre-contemplation*, where we do not feel that anything needs to change? Are we at *contemplation* where we recognize that we should begin exploring doing something different? Or, have we reached the *Action Stage*, where we are actually ready to take a deep breath and wade into uncharted territory? During the Contemplation Stage, we are looking at ourselves without make-up, our Spanx undergarments, or anything else that can create an illusion of being something we are not. Instead, we must put a critical eye on our lives and ourselves and determine what about ourselves is not working. We must then be willing to address how we would want things to be different and identify how we can go about making it happen.

A Self-Assessment
- There is something about my life I would change
- There are goals that I have wanted to achieve but still have not gone about doing so

- There are others in my life who discourage me from pursuing my goals
- I am not happy with the person I am or have become
- I recognize that there are barriers to my doing something different, but I am ready to face them

If you answered "yes" to any of the questions above, it is time to fasten your seatbelt and board the **Change Train**.

Yet, as stated in question 5, there are barriers that may be in your path. Sometimes, these are the barriers that have kept you from pursuing your Change Plan in the past. A major barrier may be that others will view you as selfish, as making a change requires taking time to focus on you, which means less time for others. Whether this involves pursuing a college degree or some career training that means less home-cooked meals or fewer late-night trysts with your significant other because you are studying or tired, or spending time at your new gym to get the body you have always wanted—it will impact those around you. In a later chapter, we will address more in-depth how this selfishness is okay, and should not be a barrier to your Change Process. Another emotional barrier may be that you are now "Bucking the System." What you have decided you want to do differently may require you to go against societal expectations. Whether you have decided that you are going to stop pushing to have children because you prefer being "Auntie of the World" to being a mommy, or you are not as concerned with material things and want to live simply—the World may not support you or understand this change.

Those in the World who may not support your change can be broken into groups:

- Skeptics
- The Jealous
- Those living vicariously

The Skeptic-This is a person who has no true understanding of how much you can accomplish. They are likely the same person who has told you in the past you were not smart enough, strong enough, or pretty enough to do (fill in the blank). This person will likely discourage you because they do not really know *you* or what you are capable of achieving. He or she will often act as a prosecuting attorney, pointing out every hole in your plan or providing a counter-argument for every argument that you give that makes change an option. When you take steps to move forward, they are often the one who will be behind you—pulling you back using terms like "too late", "unreasonable", etc. Sometimes, it is their own insecurities that they push on to you. Yet, don't let this person stop you. Even if they make a valid point, use it as an opportunity to brainstorm/problem-solve a solution, versus just giving up.

The Jealous-This person may want to be you or is upset by the opportunities that you have. Oftentimes, they do not like the life they are living. Most of us have heard the term "Misery loves company"? Well, meet Mr. or Ms. Misery. They see themselves as unhappy or dissatisfied with their current circumstances, but are too scared or feel too helpless to make a change. Sometimes, they will justify their failure to change by talking about the impossibility of it or that it is just too late. However, because you are making a change, you are taking away their excuses and making them take personal inventory. This person will talk about you behind your back and discourage your supporters from rallying behind your Change Process. When you discuss your struggle to change, they will argue reasons that you should not. Although they may have characteristics of the Skeptic, the Jealous One *knows* that you can accomplish your goal but fears what it will mean for them if you do.

The One Living Vicariously- This person is the hardest to shake, because often they are a relative. Even more difficult is the fact that they are likely to be a close relative like a parent or grandparent. This is the person who feels as if they sacrificed their time, energy, finances, and even their physical appearance (stretch marks, anyone?) to provide you with everything they wish they could have had. Instead of following the path that they so desperately wanted for themselves, you are choosing to go outside of that and pursue something that you want. You may be shown college bills, private school bills, etc demonstrating the sacrifices that *The One Living Vicariously* has made so that you can become the doctor, lawyer, ballerina, etc. that they always wanted to be. This person struggles between being proud that they have equipped you with the tools that you need to be whatever you want to be, and wanting desperately for you to become the college professor, writer, Broadway star that they couldn't. You may see this person champion your success while at the same time pointing out how you could have been more successful in the life they designed for you.

As stated earlier, change is not easy, but at times, it is necessary for us to live up to our full potential. In the

Change Process, we have to acknowledge our power to be whomever we would like in spite of opposition from society, stereotypes, or even those closest to us. We must accept that we are destined for greatness while at the same time knowing that our destiny can only be fulfilled if we put forth the effort to make an honest self-assessment, sacrifice in the short-term to meet the long-term goal, and then praise ourselves for allowing change to happen.

My Change Contract

I_____ am making a commitment to change. Although I know that change can be difficult/scary, I am resolving to do it. The change I need to make is _____
_____
_____ .

The reason(s) this change is necessary/good for me is/are _____
_____
_____
_____ .

I understand that, just because this change is good for me, there are some who will not support my change. I recognize that _____
_____ may not be supportive, but I will still move forward with my change. I also know that I can count on _____
_____ to assist me, encourage me, and be there for me as I make my change.

The barriers to my change are _____
_____ .

Because I know the barriers, I can overcome them by
_____ .

This is my pledge to myself.

Change will happen.

_____
Your Name Here

Cleaning Out Your Closet

I love the shows *Hoarders* and *Clean House*. *Hoarders* is a show that follows people with Obsessive-Compulsive Disorder (OCD) who just can't seem to get rid of anything. Their houses are full of trash and other things that most people would discard, yet they continue to hold on to them for dear life. *Clean House* is just a less disgusting version of *Hoarders* where people still have the boxes of clothes but one is unlikely to find dead cats or mildewed food in the mix. My husband will roll his eyes when I sit down to watch either of them. His reaction is understandable as, after watching an episode of either show, I will go on a cleaning spree, throwing away any item that is not nailed down or that neither he nor our oldest daughter can explain the reason for keeping. Although it is easy for me to shake my head at the people on *Hoarders* and *Clean House* because of their cluttered homes, I also had to realize that one's emotional house can be just as cluttered and that I, and other women, are not as eager to clean that one out.

I like to call this Emotional Hoarding—our tendency to not go through and throw away the emotional baggage that is cluttering up our lives. We must begin to look at what keeps us from "cleaning out our [emotional] closet".

It's time for us to take a tour of your emotional closet. We are going to go through it and look at the things that are cluttering up your space/spirit, get rid of the things that we can, and get help in organizing/dealing with those things we can't manage alone.

Our first step is the space known as:

Holding on to something that is long gone—this is the space where old relationships should go to die. Where the person we thought was the love of our life left us disillusioned, burnt out, or just left. Instead of taking it out to the trash where it belongs, we instead go through the "what ifs" over and over again. We pull this relationship out when the one that we have currently is just not going our way and make unfair comparisons. Although this is in our closet, we somehow make sure that it is sparkling clean on the side we view, with the dust of disappointment, lies, infidelity, etc. being hidden on the side against the wall. The goal is to remember the good times, while dismissing/forgetting all of the reasons that the relationship did not work out. We need to be able to reminisce, and that only works when it puts a smile on your face. This spot may also hold the songs you played, the places you went together, and old photos of "happier times"—all things you need to keep this long-dead relationship alive. We may ask those around us about this person, wondering if they are happy in their current relationship, while secretly hoping that they are not. Continuing friendships with those with whom they remain connected is essential to keeping this space in our closet, because additional pieces/tidbits need to be placed there in order to keep the space occupied. In this technological age, we may even 'Google' their name to continue to have a glimpse in to their lives, or attempt seemingly platonic relationships with them in order to remain connected to them in some small way, "just in case" and for the chance for them to ask "what if?" Yet, this space serves no purpose but to keep space filled that could be open for new adventures, new people, and healthier relationships. So, we must look at what we need to do to clean out this space in the closet

- **Acknowledge that the relationship is over**—not kind of over, not maybe over, but over. Only when we get beyond believing that some part of the relationship continues to exist can we feel okay about removing it from our emotional closet.

- **Be able to state out loud (and mean it) that the relationship was not as great as you "remember"**—there is a reason the relationship ended—whether by your actions or those of the other person. Something about it just was not right and caused it to end. If need be, for every "great" memory, write down two that were not so great. The goal is to get a realistic picture of the relationship vs. a sentimental one. Sentimental ones are those that we will often keep, while when we view the relationship in all of its stark reality, we are more likely to see the need to let it go.

- **Break up with the person**—yes, this supposedly already happened, but somewhere along the line, it got lost in your mind's translation. If you are still pining for what coulda, shoulda, woulda been—you need to get yourself to understand that the relationship is over. This may also mean literally "breaking off" the friendship you have encouraged with them. If you fostered the friendship in hopes of rekindling an intimate relationship, you are doing yourself and them a disservice.

- **Don't hunt them down**—Googling needs to be your enemy. Facebook is *not* your friend. Looking them up online out of curiousity only serves to keep the person's place in your heart and closet. Learn to be your own computer filter and stop yourself before you type in their first full name in the computer's search engine
- **Get rid of "our song", "our place", etc.**—if there is a place that you have avoided going to with your current significant other, or a song that you will not dance to with anyone because "they belonged to (insert name of ex) and that relationship." Make a point to visit that place, dance to that song, etc. with someone who means the world to you NOW. As long as you keep some things sacred to that person and that relationship, it retains a hold on you and its place in your closet

The next part of your closet is likely the Hanging Area of Regrets. This area is likely to be somewhat large and can be divided into **Regret Areas 1, 2, and 3**. I say hanging because it always seems like the items over here are dangling in front of your face, but too high up for you to reach. Here lies the things you wish you would have done, the people you wish you would have dated/married, and the places you wish you could have visited.

Let's start with **Regret Area 1**. Depending upon how fulfilled you are in your life, determines how much of your closet is taken up by this area. For some, it may be a tiny little corner, for others it might take up an entire wall. We go to this section every time we learn about the accomplishment of a friend or even worse, an enemy. We try to reach for the items to take down, but can only stare at them from a distance because they remain out of our reach. We think about how "it should have been me" or how we should have put off having our children (or never having them). This is also the place where we think about how we should have waited for "Mr. Right" vs. taking "Mr. Right Now" because we didn't want to grow old alone. For some reason, we ignore the stool sitting beside this area that may permit us to still reach for our dreams or how the racks are really broken and may not be things that we would want/need anyway.

Nicole is a 50something woman who dropped out of college to get married. Being a good Catholic, she knew that not having her child was not an option. Thirty years later, after putting all of her children through college and watching them get the degrees she failed to get, Nicole is open about her regrets. Yet, when others point out that she can still return to school and get the degree she wanted, Nicole sighs and tells them it is too late.

Nicole has chosen to wrap herself in the **Garments of Regret**. Sometimes, we don't want to reach for the stool that will still permit us to achieve our dreams. Occasionally, it is out of fear—fear that we cannot succeed or that dream achievement will not bring that longed for fulfillment. At other times, it is because the

Failed Dream Fulfillment allows us to wallow in misery that is familiar to us and provides us with the excuse needed to hold on to bitterness or to not have to live up to our potential. Regardless of what we may argue, there are many of us who enjoy our bitterness—we suck on it like a piece of sweet fruit and don't want to let it go because it would mean that we have to examine ourselves more closely and begin to make behavioral change. This bitterness may also offer us the *Cloak of Martyrdom*—something to hold over the heads of those we purport to love to instill in them feelings of guilt and make us feel powerful about how we have suffered. How many of you have heard stories from women (who make a point to say it loudly in front of their parents/kids/partners) about how much they sacrificed/gave up to be a better daughter/mother/wife? They talk about how they could have been on Broadway, a partner in the law firm, on the cover of *Ebony* magazine, or a bestselling author if they just wouldn't have given it all up to take care of parents/have children/get married? At the end of the day, the decision to not pursue our dreams lies more within us as we make the conscious effort to go after other avenues.

Area of Regret 2 might be **that which contains mistakes we feel that we have made that we continue to focus on, but do not change.** This may include remaining in a relationship that is not healthy, continuing to spend money that we do not have, or staying in a career or job that we hate. We stare at this section of the closet daily because it is an everyday part of our lives. We wonder what holds us back from cleaning out this part of the closet. Sometimes, it is those around us who should help clean it, but instead they insist that it needs to stay exactly as it is. These people may be parents or even people from our House of Worship who tell us that "God only puts on you as much as you can bear", or inform you that divorce is never acceptable—no matter if he hurts you, cheats on you, or does anything else wrong. So in this section, you may have hung a picture of your family, friends, or favorite religious symbol to assist you in fighting the urge to clean out this part of the closet. Other things hanging here may include a dollar bill to remind you that you must stay in your job for financial security, even though it is wreaking havoc on your emotional well-being. This area of Regret may require you to first remove the symbols that keep them a part of your life—including worrying about what others say, not using your faith as a means to strengthen your resolve to clean out this area but instead to maintain the status quo, or examining how you can work toward still being able to feed your family in a career/job that also feeds your spirit.

The last section of the Area of Regret, which we have called **Area of Regret 3** may hold **our sequined/ rhinestone best.** These are elements of excitement that we never experienced because we married our high school sweetheart, was the good Christian girl, or otherwise followed the Straight and Narrow Path. Often, this section is a little easier to reach. We can go to it, and pull items down to get that little bit of excitement. However, we don't notice that the sequins are poorly stitched and the rhinestones are glued on versus sewn and that we have perhaps plainer, but more durable and better-made items in the area of our closet that we frequent daily. The concept of "the grass is always greener on the other side" hangs in this section. We keep piling up the poorly made rhinestone-embossed and sequined life experiences in this area—usually with items given to us by others who wish that they lived the lives that we have. The givers of the "gifts" in this part of the closet are usually those who wish they had the stable relationship that you do, have their own bitterness with which they are dealing, or some other issue that makes them want you to leave the comfort of your existence and enter the uncertainty of their own. They will feed this part of your closet with advice that urges you to gain new male friends with whom your husband would not approve, to go hang out like someone who does not have dignity or a name to protect, or tell you what they would do if they were in your position (even though they have never been there). Yet, because we are overwhelmed by the false shininess of this part of the Area of Regret, we do not sit back and take inventory as it relates to why we stopped going to clubs, didn't date the local drug dealer, or stopped/never tried a drink. Instead, we focus on the attractiveness/excitement in the situation, not realizing that the more time we spend in this rhinestone/sequined area, the more neglected the other parts of our closet become. Then, we run the risk of others coming in and recognizing the beauty inherent in our everyday attire/lives and being more than willing to take over that part of our closet.

Evaluating the Area of Regret
- Is the item a goal that you can still achieve but might require a little sacrifice?
- If yes, are you willing to make the sacrifice— whether it is staying up late, going back to

school, leaving your house a mess, or having less money?

- Is it a goal that is realistic and should be pursued? If you are only 5'2 and have bad knees and never even played on your high school basketball team, your dream of WNBA stardom may need to be modified to something within the sports arena, instead of on the court
- Do you see this goal as leading to more happiness in your life or just more dissatisfaction?
- Is it something that is causing you or those you love to live in fear or to experience regular emotional pain? If so, what supports can you look to that may help leave the regret behind and can assist you in challenging whatever makes you feel that you have to stay?

Getting Rid of the Rhinestones

- Begin to truly look at what you missed—are the people who are still within that environment truly happy or do they envy what you have? If they want what you have, maybe the grass isn't greener.
- Those who continue to encourage your involvement in that world—are they truly looking out for your best interest, or is it a case of Misery Loves Company?
- Is wrapping yourself in the excitement worth losing whatever stability you might already have? If so, go for it, if you think you can Have your Excitement and your life, too—you might need to give pause.

The back of the closet

This is the area that we don't go. It is where we put things of which we can't let go, but don't want to see. We never go to this part of the closet, but we may continue to shove things in there. Because it is in the back, we hope that others don't notice the clutter or will politely ignore it. Yet, because it takes up space, it is always in our minds and impacts what other things (good or bad) we can fit into our closet. The idea of cleaning out this area of the closet stresses us out, leaves us feeling overwhelmed, and may cause us emotional pain. Although we try and ignore it, today we are going to take a deep breath, step in to that part of the closet, and acknowledge what is there.

The first thing you may encounter when you go to this part of the closet is *things you have done in the past of which you are ashamed*. They may range from sexual promiscuity to past substance abuse that you have not shared with those currently taking center stage in your life. Many of us have aspects of our lives that go beyond the standard regret and go into the realm of embarrassment, shame or guilt. The goal in life is that we all grow and mature, but the youthful transgressions do not go away, instead, we push them back into this part of our closet. We are too afraid to bring them out, sort through them and determine what we need to share with others. Instead, our fear and shame make us just keep them tucked away because we don't believe our explanation for them will be good enough for those who occupy our lives at this time. Sometimes, this area is also kept because we have told lies or half-truths that make it so that we cannot risk bringing these objects out into the light because someone may see them before we can figure out how to remove them.

Sometimes, we may even share some of them in our testimonies with others who have done the same thing, but still can't bring ourselves to share with the world.

I remember reading about how some women would say that, when telling your spouse/partner your number of sexual partners to divide by two because they would not understand or be accepting of the amount of their sexual experience. Or the person who had a history of substance use in which she made decisions under the influence—and now that sobriety has been in place, wishes to forget the past, but just cannot.

Going a little deeper in this back of the closet, we may find that it gets cold because we have needed to freeze our hearts to be able to function. This area is dark because we do not want to shine a light on what exists there. Instead, we reach our hand in every now and then, but never try to pull anything out. Some days, we may even find that this part of the closet is spilling out into the rest of the space and we quickly try to shove it back in before it sees the light of day or we fear that it may somehow come into contact with other parts of our closet and contaminate them.

Studies vary, but even conservative estimates suggest that 1 in 6 women will be sexually assaulted in their lifetime[3]. With numbers such as those, sexual abuse is likely to be in the back of many of our closets. Although we may push the sexual abuse into the very back of our closets, it is likely to not stay there. Sexual abuse has been shown to have significant impact on us. When lecturing on one occasion, I compared sexual abuse to a cancer. It starts in one part of the body, and spreads

---

3   http://www.rainn.org/statistics downloaded 2/25/10

throughout. It affects your mind—including the way you view yourself. It also impacts the body—either by body image or the physical effects of the abuse. Our hearts are affected, as well, because we are likely to view others with suspicion or close off parts of ourselves because we don't want to experience the pain again; or we believe that we are tainted goods and not worthy of love. In my work as a psychologist, the impact of abuse on women has been clear:

- Depression
- Difficulty in developing intimate relationships
- Sexual issues
- Self-concept
- Anxiety
- Physical trauma
- PTSD
- Guilt
- Substance abuse
- Isolation
- Increased risk of future victimization

This part of our closet is often the most difficult to clean as the impact of the abuse may have seeped into the flooring and stained the walls. It has become a part of the landscape of our closet, and when we dare to look in this part, feelings of helplessness and anger may overcome us as we view cleaning this part of the closet as an impossible task. So, instead of cleaning it up, we push more items in front of it, hoping that, one day, we will have the strength to actually begin to clean it. Although other parts of our closet are capable of being cleaned by us, alone, or with the assistance of our friends, this part of our closet is likely to need more experienced helpers. Such helpers may include a supportive group of female friends who have experience cleaning out this section of their own closets. They will likely talk about the ways they were able to bravely begin to clean this back part of their closet. Also, we may consult books written about abuse, or if need be, we must open ourselves up to the idea of seeking the services of professionals who have worked with sexual abuse survivors and who understand the depression, difficulty in relationships, and trauma that was experienced. When we begin to clean out this part of the closet, we may find that the layers of hurt, anger, fear, etc. go even deeper than we thought—but we must remember that at least 1 in 6 of us have this in a part of our closet and many have been able to go through the process of healing/cleaning it.

Resources for the back of the closet
www.rainn.org
www.darkness2light.org

Examining My Closet

The following things are in my closet

1. _____
2. _____
3. _____
4. _____

The reasons I am having difficulty cleaning out my closet are

1. _____
2. _____
3. _____
4. _____
5. _____

The people/resources I need to help me really begin the cleaning of my closet process are

1. _____
2. _____
3. _____
4. _____

Disclaimer: This chapter is not intended for anyone experiencing domestic violence. Instead, it is for those in relationships that appear to not serve a benefit for the person reading this, but does not have aspects of power and control by one person over another, fear, abuse or violence. For more comprehensive information on the unique aspects of domestic violence within an intimate relationship and to find resources for those experiencing domestic violence, the reader is encouraged to go to the following:

Ohio Domestic Violence Network
800-934-9840
www.odvn.org
National Coalition Against Domestic Violence
(303) 839-1852
www.ncadv.org

Toxic Relationships

I remember calling my mother the Tuesday before Thanksgiving. I had been visiting with my then-boyfriend who had decided that he would choose that holiday weekend to propose. Calling my mother with the news, I was surprised at her response. She informed me that she had never been prouder of me than she was at that moment. Such a response threw me as I went back over accomplishments that I had in my life up to that point. Graduating salutatorian from high school, publishing my first short story while in high school, summa cum laude graduation from Wilberforce University, getting my doctorate degree and becoming a psychologist. However, out of all of my true accomplishments, my mother was on the telephone informing me that what made her the most proud was that someone had asked me to marry them. Yet, I realize that such a statement was a commentary on the state of being female. Often, we are reared to value relationships and to want to be a part of them. In previous generations, even our pursuit of higher education was deemed a plan to get a "Mrs." degree versus a bachelor's. The goal of attending college was not to gain an education, but to find a suitable husband. As young girls, we are given dolls and taught to be mothers—again valuing the need for relationships and to care for others, while our brothers are given toys that build cities and then destroy them. It is no wonder that, when you watch television shows such as MSNBC Lock-Up, the visiting rooms at the male prisons are filled with women maintaining or undertaking relationships with inmates, while the women's visiting rooms are often lonely places. In this emphasis on relationships, we as women will often suffer through those that may not be good for us because we were taught that relationships encompass our proudest moments.

When I visited my doctor for a prenatal visit, I noticed a regular garbage can and a separate one that had a bright red bag with a biohazard sign. Looking at that bag, I realized that the hospital was doing something we often fail to do—it was separating what is toxic from what was normal, even in items that were to be discarded. Looking at that, I wondered why we fail to do the same in our everyday lives. Why do we not separate from situations/people in our lives that are toxic?

- In defining toxic relationships, I like the definition, "containing or being poisonous material especially when capable of causing death or serious debilitation"

- extremely harsh, malicious, or harmful [4]

Breaking the definition down further, we get:
- Toxic does not mean that it will "kill you" in small doses
- Exposure to toxins over time will wreak havoc on the individual
- Toxins are not good for you, but we often can handle them in small increments

When a relationship is toxic, it causes you problems
- Mentally
- Physically
- Emotionally
- Spiritually

Let's examine toxic relationships by breaking them down into two groups—platonic friendships and intimate relationships.

Toxic Friendships

Confession: Being a strong feminist, I cringed when the book <u>Men are from Mars, Women are from Venus</u> burst on to the literary scene. My annoyance stemmed from the book's premise than men and women are genetically different and would therefore react in different ways in relationships. Yet, although I would still argue with the belief that "men are men" and "women are women", which pushes for excuses and negates personal responsibility in relationship choices/ behaviors, I have come to believe that, even if not "wired" differently, women are at least encouraged

---

4 Websters' dictionary on-line http://www.merriam-webster.com/ dictionary Downloaded 2/29/08

to value friendships/relationships, where men may not. Such a statement should not be taken as scientific fact, but more so based on life experience. Because of our need for sister-friends, it seems as if we as women also run a higher risk of toxic friendships.

I had a cousin who was like a best friend to me. We were practically raised together. Our mothers encouraged our bond. However, like clockwork, she would always provoke a major fallout over something minor. At that time, she would say anything to hurt my feelings, spread my business to others, and encourage all of our relatives and mutual friends to "hate me, too." Yet, the problem was not her behavior, but the fact that I would "take her back" (wearily) and continue our friendship. After one such blow up, my husband cautiously asked why I continued to hold on to that friendship. He could understand maintaining the family tie, but not the friendship. He went on to tell me how he would have let a friend go after the first blow up. His comment made me wonder why, we as women, have such a hard time letting go of friendships that are bad for us?

Yes, we value relationships. Yes, we love our sister-friends. However, why do we cling to those friends who demonstrate over and over that they are not good for us? At what point do we, as my husband said, "just let it go"?.

Reasons why we stay in toxic friendships
1. The good in the friendship outweighs the bad

As women, we focus on the "good times" in the relationship. We remember how that person was fun, was there for us, etc. However, if the good times are a distant memory and our mental images of those times was when we were in bellbottoms, had jheri curls, or were playing in a sandbox, then they occurred too long ago to justify the friendship. Another thing to look at—if you find yourself having to remind yourself of the good times when your friend is being emotionally exhausting, it may be time to reevaluate it

2. We feel bad about "breaking up"

"Breaking up is hard to do" was a popular song for a reason. It has a true message. Discontinuing friendships can be difficult. It is uncomfortable to hurt someone's feelings—even someone who didn't mind hurting yours. Sometimes, we continue a relationship to avoid the discomfort of ending it. However, in our goal to not hurt someone else, we are causing pain in our own lives—that associated with sharing space with someone who is suffocating us or consistently stressing us out.

3. Fear what others will think

Public perception is important—there is no denying it. If that were not the case, we would not spend as much money on clothes, make-up, jewelry, hair, nails, or cars. On some level, we all want to be seen as wonderful people. It is not uncommon for those with whom we have toxic friendships to share other friends with us. It is even worse when the "friend" saves his/her toxic tendencies for only us—which makes it more difficult to explain our reluctance to continue the friendship with those in our shared social circle.

No one wants to be viewed as "the bad friend"—which can become the case when no one else is experiencing the same toxicity/venom that you get.

We must begin to not worry about what the rest of our shared circle will think of us. If they begin to be critical of us or exclude us because we choose to not fully interact with the one that was toxic for us, perhaps they also have some "toxic tendencies", and may not be good for us, either.

On the other hand, they may demonstrate respect for our decision, especially when we do not attempt to get them to take sides. They may surprise us and be willing to balance their relationship with us and with the toxic friend, allowing a better appreciation of that healthier relationship.

4.   They are family or like family, and you can never turn your back on family

Working with children who are often referred by Child Protective Services, I have often been in the unenviable position of helping children develop realistic expectations of absentee parents. It is amazing how a child can calmly come to the realization that they can love a parent, while also moving back from that relationship. Yet, we as adults struggle with this. How many times have we shuddered when we thought about a family member, high school friend, neighbor from back home because they seemed to drain the life out of us? However, we continued gk to stay because "they are family." We must get to the point of accepting that there are levels of relationships. You may not be able to totally disown that sister/brother/cousin/aunt/even mother, but setting stronger parameters around the relationship may be healthier for you and them. For one, it begins to show them that they cannot continue to harm or disappoint those around them and have the relationship go on as normal. Two, it permits you to meet the family obligation, while at the same time saying "See you at the family reunion" instead of on a daily basis.

Activity: Is your friendship toxic?

- Instead of congratulating you on your successes, the friend either:
  a. Downplays it as not a big deal. For example, "Sure, it's a masters' degree, but it's not like you earned a doctorate" or "A promotion? Great, but they aren't paying you any more money."
  b. Insists upon one-upping you. For example "glad you got a car, but I'm buying a_____(fill in the blank with any car that is more expensive than the one you have purchased).
  c. They just can't be happy for you. For example "so? Who cares about _____"(fill in the blank with your accomplishment).

- Discourages you from pursuing your dream— now, this does not include the friend who discourages you from doing something that you may regret later (for example, submitting your picture for a centerfold in a magazine, trying your hand at stripping to make quick money, etc)

- Instead of being supportive of you, they always seem to be in competition with you.

- Claim friendship, but are quick to think the worst of you in a situation. For example "She must not care" instead of "You must have just gotten busy."

- Are openly critical of you to others—if this friend tells you how so-and-so called you out of your name so many times, you must begin to wonder what made so-and-so comfortable to say such things about you in front of your girl?

- Want *what* you have, not something *like* yours—this does not include that bad Michael Kors purse you got for an unbelievable price at the outlet. Instead, this refers to (a) your man (b) your job or even (c) always seems to try and holler at the people you have your eye on

- Attempt to rally others to dislike you when you are in conflict vs. dealing with the conflict head on. As people, we likely will have disagreements, but must the disagreement become an issue for your entire social circle?

- Piggybacking on #7, when you disagree, the friend's goal is to hurt you—not just resolve the issue. The friend may even throw up every bad memory/life story that you shared with them back in your face

- You sigh when you see their name on caller ID because you know there is going to be some drama

- The relationship feels like a bumpy roller coaster ride that you wish you could get off

If you answered "yes" to even one of these, you should evaluate whether or not the friendship is good for you vs. just being good for the other person.

Toxic Intimacy

Like many women, mistakes are made in relationships. In looking at my friends and friends-of-friends, few, if any, tell me that they have either (1) not dated someone they wish they had not (2) made a mistake in a dating relationship.

Yet, toxic relationships go beyond mere mistakes and can range from the lyrics of Lauryn Hill's Ex-Factor:

….and when I try to walk away
You hurt yourself to make me stay—
This is crazy

This extends all the way to situations that can be and are deadly for women.

Do not get me wrong. Dating and/or marriage can be a good thing. Although, I never bought into the idea that someone should "complete me," the idea that a partner could complement/enhance me was within my realm of understanding. Yet, in our search for completion, we often let others define us.

Hope/Waiting

I spent all of my time waiting for you
Waiting by the phone
Wondering when you'd come home
Cause I didn't want to be alone
Listening to the melancholic tone

Of Henderson on the saxophone
Lulling me to an uneasy slumber
Waiting for you
Waiting for you to see
That you fit me
Like cornbread and black-eyed peas
On New Year's Eve
And I wanted to be your resolution
So I kept on Waiting
Waiting for you
Waiting for the time, when you'd realize
That my love is something to recognize
Not trivialize
Cause you can look in my eyes
And with a harsh glance, I die inside
Withering in the loss that is your approval
And I need that more than air
Waiting for you
Waiting for you to cherish me
Like my daddy said I should be
Or he would have if he wasn't a mystery
And I wrap myself in your masculinity
To be able to express my femininity
And put down the independent woman everyone
*   else sees*
Cause I wanted to be your concubine and lay at
*   your feet*
Like I am a faithful servant
And you are my priest
Worshipping at the altar of you
Waiting for you
I spent my time waiting patiently
Not understanding that by doing so, I lost
Me

The chance to revel in my own mystique
Or see if I could accomplish goals that I would seek
To love me for what I was and could be
Cause I spent all my time
Waiting for you
To define
Me
—-TMD 2004

How many of us have spent a large amount of our lives waiting for a boyfriend/husband/partner to become the person we want/need them to be? How about trying hard to be something that we are not in order to live up to their expectations? More importantly, once we recognize that either of the above scenarios is occurring, why do we continue to stay?

A highly-educated friend of mine once sat me down and complained about her boyfriend's lack of drive, his financial instability, and emotional immaturity. This sister-friend had excellent credit, owned her own home, and was steadily climbing up the corporate ladder. Later on, she married him and still complained that he lacked drive, couldn't manage money, and was childish. Basically, nothing had changed. Being that he stayed the same, the assumption would be that she should not complain or be surprised because *he was exactly the person she dated*. He would be within his right to assume that she was content with whom he was—because that is whom she chose to marry.

On a similar note, some of us often "settle"—feeling that we do not deserve the blessings intended for us. Instead of holding out for the person who meets our needs, embodies some of our wants, and does not have any of our "deal-breakers", our patience wears thin and we make *Mr. Right Now* into *Mr. Forever*. In doing so, we often ignore the early warning signs that may tell us that the relationship is headed toward disaster. In such instances, toxic can be more than emotionally deadly, but physically as well.

Jennifer, a college-educated 40 something African-American woman shared her story of a toxic marital relationship.

I was married to the man of my dreams, or so I thought. He was really a nightmare. It started out normal enough. He was kind, attentive, and a good provider. He loved God, me, his children and mine. He practically paid for the entire wedding!! Soon afterward, his real agenda came out. He always spoke negatively of his son's mother; how unfit she was, her habits, her life. Looking back, he probably had a lot to do with it. He really needed a mother for his son. I agreed to let his son move in with us. The little boy was a terror. He grew up with little guidance and was basically raising himself. Once he moved in everything was up to me, and he was gone more and more. I soon learned of his addictions: gambling, drugs and other women. It reminded me of my father. In my family, my parents have been married for 48 years, my grandparents 53 years, and divorce was unheard of for us. The ones who didn't get along simply led separate lives, but stayed married. So who was I to break this tradition? I prayed that I would be strong enough to leave. I prayed for financial fitness to be on my own. I prayed for strength to walk away. Then God began to reveal things to me. He said, "Look around". "When's the last time he paid a bill?" "You got this apartment on your own, you just bought a new car without him and the furniture you got on your own." "He's actually in your way." So, I called my mother and father and children together, and told them my plan. What I thought was going to be a long fight turned into a celebration. My parents rented a U-haul that morning and we went to the apartment and cleaned it out. I didn't take anything that wasn't mine, just my stuff and my children's stuff. When we were done, the only things left in the apartment were his clothes and a television. I even took the cable wires and box because I was paying for that, too. I thought I was going to cry but I had cried enough when I was with him. I never looked back. 3 months later I bought a house. My house!!!!

As Jennifer's story illustrates, sometimes, we believe that the toxic relationship is something we deserve. Although our family and friends may warn us about the relationship and encourage us to go, we let the toxic person "get in our head" and begin to believe that the relationship is what we need. However, once we are able to remove ourselves from the situation, we begin to identify the attributes that we have and can then permit ourselves to heal and be ready for the relationships we ought to have.

So, what is a "deal-breaker"? Well, it varies from one woman to the next, but simply means any characteristic with which you cannot live. For some, a deal-breaker may be someone who has children. For others, it may be someone who has been married before, has a criminal record, etc. A deal-breaker is *your own*. We must not feel bad about saying something is non-negotiable for us. We must not give in to those around us telling us that we are too bourgeoisie, picky, etc. At the end of the day, when the door closes and the lights dim, we are left with the person we have chosen, so we must choose wisely.

Exercise—Yes, maybe, or a deal-breaker?

Write down a list of must-haves for an intimate relationship. These are not things that would "be nice", but those that are essential for you to envision a long-term, positive relationship. For example, tall may be nice for my beautician who is Amazonian, but it is not a requirement. Someone who has a good relationship with her son is essential. Don't be shy and don't worry about what others would say or would believe that you should not be so picky. Remember, this is *your life* and you should get what you need.

Now, write a list entitled "that would be nice". These would be the characteristics/attributes that would make you sing/hum because they are like an extra scoop of ice cream, not needed, but makes the dessert even more delicious.

Next, give up your deal-breakers. Again, these are the characteristics that would make your relationship head down the toxic or bad road. These would sink or should sink your relationship before it even starts. Characteristics that would make you seethe with anger/resentment should go here. Also, any of the things that you will throw up in your man's face when he makes you angry (as reasons you should not have been with him in the first place) also belong here.

Lastly, look at the lists you developed. It's time for self-inspection. Do you possess any of your deal-breakers? If so, it may be time to re-evaluate your standards, or seriously begin to work on self-change. (Please see the chapter entitled, "Change is Good").

Myths that Keep Us in Intimate Toxic Relationships
1. "I invested too much time"

It is interesting when I have run across women who will complain about the state of their marriage/intimate relationships. They will moan about infidelity, irresponsibility, and other issues. Yet, when asked why they stay, a common response is "I've invested too much time in this relationship" or "we've already been together [insert years]."

We need to begin looking at our relationships like we look at our money. For instance, look at it as if we put our paycheck in a savings account every month with the plan being that we were going to retire with that money. Our understanding being that, as long as we put more in, the bank will hold up its end by paying us interest.

However, if every month, our money decreased and the more we put in, the more the bank took, within a few months, we would withdraw our money and take it elsewhere. So, why don't we do that with something more precious than mere dollar bills? Why don't we show as much consideration/reverence/ concern for our minds, love, and bodies? We continue to stay in unwedded bliss with someone we have been "engaged" to for 10 years, won't set a wedding date, have his kids, and even pay his bills— all for nothing tangible in return. At what point do we look at our Love Bank, realize we've invested foolishly, and withdraw our funds before its value decreases even more——or worse, we forget its true value?

2. "My love will change him"
If love alone could change someone, we would not have divorce, or children incarcerated. A person changes because they *choose* to change. They decide something is not working for them. If you continue to stay and put up with the behaviors, why would they do something different? True, there are stories of people choosing to change because their partner wanted them to—but it usually occurs after an ultimatum. However, if you make ultimatums more than you make breakfast and they do not work, the likelihood is that the other person is content with being the person they are. You can either accept it, or make the decision to go.

3. "I just need to change and it will all work out."
Sometimes, we believe that if we changed who we are, then he would love us more, treat us right, etc. Yet, just as we must accept the person with whom we are in a relationship, they must also accept us. A disclaimer—if you have somehow changed physically, emotionally, intellectually from the moment when he chose you or vice versa, it is not about you changing now, but the need to revert back to who you

were in the beginning. If this is not desirable for you or doable for you, perhaps the relationship is not, either.

4. *"I need to stay for my (kids/family, etc)."*

There was a young lady I knew once whose father of her children was physically and emotionally abusive towards her. When he became angry, he would tell others that the children were not his. He also stole from her and had been violent towards her in front of their children. When I asked her why she continued to stay, she reported that the kids needed to be with both parents. So, I posed the question to her "Since we model relationships for our children, what would you say if your daughter chose to be in a relationship like yours?"

In our quest to maintain intact homes or to keep the father of our children involved, we will often sacrifice ourselves—however, we do not seem to realize that we are also sacrificing our children's chances to witness a healthy relationship.

If you are still unsure if a relationship is toxic, think of the relationship that you are questioning. Circle any of the feelings below that you often experience in this relationship.

- Emotionally drained
- Hopeless
- Tired
- Angry
- Used
- Paranoid
- Stressed
- Resentful

The more of these you feel, the more likely that the relationship has some level of toxicity and you need to determine whether or not it is good for you.

Sometimes, unhealthy intimate relationships go to an entirely different level of toxicity. According to the Bureau of Justice Statistics, in 2008, 552,000 females experienced non-fatal violent victimization by an intimate partner.[1] Even though many will argue that men can also be the victims in violent intimate relationships, according to the National Council Against Domestic Violence's Fact Sheet, 1in 4 women will experience domestic violence in their lifetime[2]. In addition, it goes on to report that 85% of victims of domestic violence are women. Where reasons for toxic intimate relationships may be based in selfishness, unrealistic expectations, etc., those within a domestic violence relationship are based upon power and control. The need for our partner to not just have some say in our lives and our emotions, but to actively be in charge of them to the point that we may feel as if we no longer can exercise any control over our lives for fear of what will happen if we attempt to do so. Sometimes, we may simply choose to view our relationship as toxic, while it may actually go to the next level of being one that is physically or emotionally violent.

What are the signs of a domestic violence relationship? According to the Ohio Domestic Violence Network's in their <u>Helping A Victim of Domestic Violence: A guide for family and friends</u> booklet. Examples of domestic violence include:
- Verbal-Name-calling, threats to hurt or kill, or put-downs

- Emotional-isolation from others, criticism, blaming
- Financial-controlling the money, destroying property, running up debts
- Sexual-constant sexual demands, forcing unwanted sexual acts
- Physical-pushing, kicking, punching

Often, as friends of those in domestic violence relationships, we may push our sister-friends to end these toxic relationships just like we would any other form. However, where we can just say "let it go" in lower levels of toxic relationships, those that rise to the level of domestic violence are often harder to "just leave." As a goal of the violent partner is often to isolate our sister-friends from us in order to increase their control, we must balance between letting the sister-friend know that they can leave with the understanding of the danger and difficulty inherent in doing so. First we must keep from allowing the isolation to occur. The Ohio Domestic Violence Network offers some advice including

- Listening without judging-Let her know that you are there for her and let her talk.
- Trust her knowledge-our sister-friends know their relationships better than we do, we must trust their judgment regarding when they feel the safest
- Do not make choices for her-abusers often limit our sister-friends' abilities to make choices for themselves...do not be like the abusers
- Learn about community resources-find out what resources are available in the community

to help those experiencing domestic violence relationships. This will help you become educated on domestic violence so you can assist your sister-friends as well as permitting you to provide resources when she is ready

• Encourage her to develop a safety plan

In our struggle to be there for our sister-friends, we must also come to terms with what may cause her to stay. It is often easy to say we would just leave. Yet, we must begin to ask ourselves what causes our sister-friends to stay and begin to help them address these concerns.

My sister Sonya had finally decided to leave her abuser. After three children including two fathered by her abuser, countless calls to the police due to domestic violence, she had decided to take the children and relocate with our other sister to South Carolina. She washed clothes and packed all day as our other sister sat nervously in the kitchen encouraging her to finally make the move. Sonya was murdered by her abuser that night. She did not make it to her 26th birthday.

Oftentimes, women will stay in domestic violence relationships because they fear what will happen if they choose to leave. Even when we decide that we are ready to end a toxic intimate relationship, it is not always easy. Sometimes, our partner is not as willing to permit us to move on. In 2007, intimate partners committed 14% of all homicides in the United States, with women females making up 70% of those killed.[3] When choosing to leave a toxic relationship that is abusive, a woman may, with good reason, be frightened by what the abuser will do now that the relationship is ending.

Tabitha, a survivor of a toxic relationship who is beginning a program to help domestic violence survivors, shared her story and offers advice:

As a survivor of domestic violence, I know that having an active safety plan in place is relevant and crucial for survival. Ten years ago when I exited my abusive relationship, it was when things were calm and he seemed to think everything was ok, (honeymoon state). Once my mind was set on leaving I began to slowly send pertinent items to a relative in another state. He was not aware of this. I told my children only a couple of days prior to leaving just in case he asked them questions. I spoke with the school and let them know what my intentions were as well as my employer. The day I left, he went to work and I sent the children to school, and I shopped for last minute things, picked up my children, left everything behind, and made my move. I have never looked back since. I now work at a school and I help young students with issues within the family, send them to appropriate resource facilities and help them with transition. If a victim is looking to exit an abusive relationship; having a safety plan which includes clothing, important numbers, keys, cell phone, and a safe location to go to would be a good start. The bag should always be packed and ready to go, but hidden in a safe spot unknown to the abuser.

Moving to Healthy

Now that we know what we should not look for in a relationship, what are the things that are necessary in a healthy one? Once we know that toxic relationships are problematic, what do we need to do to allow ourselves to move towards the healthy relationships we deserve?

- **Believe that you deserve a healthy relationship** - We must begin to believe that we deserve better than what we have experienced. Sometimes, this means looking outside of your family, friends, and community for an example of what a relationship should be like. Just because you have been reared in a home full of violence, a community in which women were not valued, or associate with people who have doubted your worth, does not mean that such relationships are the ones you deserve.

- **A little bit of selfishness** - It is okay to want someone to please you, to want and need people around you who will be your personal cheerleaders. In toxic relationships, you have surrounded yourself with those who beat you down emotionally and sometimes physically, so why not have someone in your life who holds you in high esteem?

- **Appropriate boundaries** - Someone told me once that "you can't choose your family" as they sighed and rolled their eyes in defeat about the chaos that their family members regularly brought into their lives. I looked at her and added "but you can choose how much contact you have with them." It is okay to say "see you at the family reunion" and not have more frequent contact with family members who are toxic. It is likely that you may either set an example that others in the family will follow— making the family member engage in some self-examination.

- **Realistic Expectations** - No relationship is perfect. If your goal is someone who will never get on your nerves or never do/say something you don't like—you may want to even stay away from yourself, because no one will do everything you want.
- **A good dose of pessimism** - Get rid of the "I can change them", "things will get better" mentality. If a relationship is a problem, you should not have to constantly sweat it out hoping that it will get better. If the relationship is worth it, yes, put in some time and problem solve. However, if that does not work, holding on for years hoping that a miracle will occur is just wasting your time.

Affirmation for Ending Toxic Relationships

I am a wonderful woman who deserves only positive things from those around me. I deserve to be happy, to breathe easily, to love and be loved. Reciprocity is important to me and I cannot allow myself to give and never receive. If my relationship causes me to be tired, afraid, feel hopeless, or otherwise "stuck", then it is not truly a relationship but indentured servitude and I am not a slave

---

1 U.S. Department of Justice (September 2009). Bureau of Justice Statistics Selected Findings: Female Victims of Violence.

2 http://www.ncadv.org/files/DomesticViolenceFactSheet(National).pdf Downloaded 7/5/10

3 ibid

Toxic Relationships

In this chapter, I have learned that some people in my life are or have the potential to be, toxic to me. Those people have caused me the following _____ _____.

Although it is going to be difficult to end those relationships, I know that I need to because _____ _____ _____ _____ _____ _____.

I feel _____ about ending those relationships because _____ _____ _____. However, in engaging in my process of self-reflection, I know that I need to end them. If I am concerned that my relationship involves domestic violence, I will seek out resources in my community to assist me in the ending of that relationship because I must take in to consideration my safety.

I deserve to be appreciated, loved, and respected in my relationships with others. If those in my life are not able to do so, I understand that I must make room in my life for those who can.

Too Blessed to Be Stressed

Having grown up in the Church, I was accustomed to hearing the phrase "I'm blessed" being used very frequently. It was not uncommon for someone to state they were "blessed' or "favored". As women, we are "blessed" and must begin to embrace the blessing, regardless of the toxic relationships in which we have been entangled, the changes we have gone through, or what has been buried in our closets. Prior to being able to be open to receiving such blessings, we must first acknowledge that it is "stress" that keeps us from being able to "embrace the blessing."

One day, I asked my husband what he would change about me if he could. He laughed in his "you are not going to like what I have to say" way and responded simply, "I would want you to stress less." How many of us have heard that from our loved ones or just know it for ourselves?

So, what exactly is stress?

Stress is anything that throws the body off-balance. Stress can appear in both physical and emotional forms. In the physical, it can be actual stress or strain that we put on our bodies due to over-exertion, poor eating habits, or putting in our bodies things that do not belong there (i.e., drugs, alcohol, cigarettes, etc.). These stressors are easily noticed and diagnosed by those around us. They more than likely note that we walk different, complain of physical aches, or look unhealthy in a way that no amount of make-up or clothing can mask. How many of us have found ourselves trying to juggle careers, family, and friends, only to find that our muscles are sore for no reason or that, no matter the amount of sleep we get, we are still fatigued? Oftentimes, when we ignore the emotional signs of stress, our bodies will take over and demand that we recognize that we need to develop a better way to deal with whatever is overwhelming us. Some have called this phenomenon "the body breaking down". Yet, breaking down may not be the right phrase, instead it may be simply the body insisting that we "pay attention" and acknowledge that something has to change.

Other times, the stress is not as easily noticed because it is internalized/emotional. This is the stress that goes on in our minds. It is the place where we hold our fears/worries and try not to let them out so that they do not worry or cause fear in others. Sometimes, we are justified in our stress as it can be a warning sign that we must take some action before something even worse occurs. How many of us have been stressed by a job because of layoffs, not being appreciated, or simply being overlooked? This stress may be a sign that we are not in a work environment that is conducive to our emotional health and it is time to leave it. However, at other times, stress can be an over-reaction to some perceived impending doom or situation over which we have little or no control.

There was a young man that I had taken under my wing a long time ago. I decided that I would go through the process of finishing the raising of him and become the happy (yet fabulously young-looking) grandmother when he became a man. However, I found myself being called off of my job when he would curse out teachers and going to meetings to beg for him to remain in school/on the basketball team/etc. The situation stressed me. One day, he looked at me and told me that he had to sell drugs/hang out with the wrong crowd/skip school (you fill in the blank) because "I have to look out for myself." It was in that moment that I realized that, at 16 years of age, he had decided that he was going to ignore the positives in his life and our relationship, and instead wanted to go down a path that I would not have chosen for him. In spite of my ongoing love, I had to take a deep breath and realize that I could no longer stress over the decisions that he was making. I could continue to love him, attempt to guide him, and be there for him, but I could not control him and should stop stressing because of it.

In some cases, the stress is not even there, but is more so what we fear will occur, so we ruminate about it. We keep going over and over it in our minds and just can't let it go.

Some of the most common stressors in the lives of women are:

- Living up to expectations of others
- Finances
- Education/career planning
- Relationships

Living up to the expectations of others

From the moment we are born, our parents have plans for us. They look at us and decide if they want us to be a good mother, wife, career woman, etc. We are reared to follow these roles and pushed to excel in the areas that are important to those raising us. From the beginning, we work to live up to the expectations others have for us. In our quest to please, we often will become anxious when we feel that we are letting others down. This internalization of worry can lead to sleepless nights, thinking over and over how we need to fix the problem, and physical ailments as we realize that we cannot meet whatever expectation or task others have for us. Being a psychologist, I have administered psychological tests to others, including those that address anxiety/stress. I remember one measure where the level of anxiety was based upon feeling that one cannot or does not live up to the expectations of significant others.

On the flipside, we may also be stressed by the fact that we choose to be what others want us to become. How many of us have married people we did not want, chosen careers that we did not like, or moved/remained in cities that we would not have selected all to please those around us? Spending our lives replaying the choices we believe were thrown upon us and feeling as if we cannot escape them is also stress-inducing.

Attempting to live up to the perceptions of others may not involve our own presentation, but may be due to feeling as if the failures of those around us are inherently ours. When those in our lives are addicted to drugs, having children by multiple fathers or otherwise living in a way that society has deemed unacceptable, we may choose to make their problem behavior our own. We will choose to stress over the mistakes they are making, believing that we are being judged by their actions.

Sybil is almost 40 and fabulous. She has raised her own children and provided a comfortable home for them. However, she continues to stress about the life her drug-addicted father is living. Although her father has not "hit rock bottom" and continues to be immersed in the drug culture, Sybil finds herself lying awake at night stressing over ways to force her father in to sobriety. Sybil has also been open about feelings of embarrassment at seeing her father progress in his addiction in spite of Sybil's own attempts to intervene.

Sybil has permitted someone else's stressor to become her own embarrassment. While her father remains unready to make the commitment to sobriety, Sybil has filled the role of co-dependent and is living the stressor with him.

We all suffer from "what will they think?" syndrome. We want others to view us as capable women who have it together. Yet, we cannot control the behaviors of those around us, but we view their actions as a reflection of ourselves. We must stop letting the embarrassment or problems of others become our own. No one is saying that we must step away and not continue to offer support and love to those who mean the world to us, but if they are unwilling to take the help, we need to take a deep breath and tell ourselves:

They are not ready to receive the support I have to offer. I cannot continue to have sleepless nights, not eat, neglect myself emotionally or financially in hopes that they will be ready. I do not have control over anyone but myself. Therefore, I have the ability to not stress with the knowledge that I will be here whenever they are ready to face their issues or make changes. In the meantime, I need to step away or I will not be emotionally healthy enough to help them when the time comes.

Finances.

In today's economy, coupled with society's view that "more is better", we feel pressured to **"compete with the Joneses"**. The Joneses are usually that one friend, family member, or acquaintance who seems to have it all financially. They own the car you wish you could afford, send their kids to the school whose brochure you have on the refrigerator hoping that the tuition will go down, are living in the house you envy, or shop for clothes at places in whose windows you can only browse. Whether or not one covets what is owned by the Joneses, most of us can at least identify them in our lives.

There was one woman who had decided to not attend college and be a stay-at-home mom. While others around her went off to school and pursued careers, she was content to remain in the home rearing her wonderful children. However, as her friends stopped being broke college students and became businesswomen, she found herself wanting the financial lives they led. Looking at her working-class husband whom she had always adored, she began demanding that they needed to keep up with her college-educated friends. In her pursuit of their American Dream, she found herself heavily in debt and driving a car she could ill-afford. In her pursuit of Competing with the Joneses, she lost sight of what made her happy before all of this. Now she was experiencing stress due to dealing with bill collectors for items that she never believed she needed in the first place.

We also stress about finances due to our need to Make It Right.

Talking to Chrissie, a 20-something mother of boys, I discussed with her and her husband how they had often done without a lot growing up. Their parents did not have the money to permit them to wear the latest fashions or have the latest hairstyles. Therefore, they made a commitment to make sure that their own children never experienced the discomfort associated with being among the Not Haves. However, Chrissie also acknowledged the financial strain that could come with clothing growing boys and the extra hours of work she and her husband put in to keep their boys in the latest styles. In speaking with her, Chrissie admitted to the stress, but also reported that it was manageable and that she was willing to endure it so that her sons would not feel the stress of not being able to Compete with the Joneses.

Another stressor associated with finances is that of **Not Being On the Same Page.** How many of us have set financial goals for ourselves, only to see that our partner is not holding up their end of the bargain, putting more pressure on us to make the plan a reality? My brother, who is a pastor of a church, counseled my husband and I before our marriage. He bluntly asked if we had discussed finances and our financial goals. According to him, financial problems were one of the leading strains in marriages. Yet, we often do not choose to have The Money Conversation, either fearing that we will be viewed as Gold Diggers, or that we will not like the answer we get. Yet, if we continue the relationship, the financial problems that may plague our partner become ours as well. Whether he is not working and we have to figure out how to manage the bills, he chooses to spend rather than save and we wonder about being able to retire, or on the extreme end, he is unable to assist in providing for the home due to incarceration or illness. Because of embarrassment, this form of financial stress is one that we will often hide from those around us. We will claim he is working while slipping him our credit card so he can appear to be paying the bill, will return items that we needed for the home to compensate for that expensive electronic equipment or clothing that he splurged to purchase, or not even acknowledge his illness or incarceration. Putting all the financial responsibility on our own shoulders, especially in a situation in which it should not be, is hard to handle.

Education/Career Planning

Everyone is expected to have a game plan; at least that is what I was told growing up. Even in the 6th grade, we were asked to make a clock, list what happened in the past, what is current, and then make a plan for our future. In elementary school and junior high, the question of, "What do you want to be when you grow up?" is a common one. In fact, by high school, we are expected to have our game plans in place. If not, we are overwhelmed with an abundance of college recruiters and military recruiters, trying to help us decide our education or career plan. At some point in time, it was determined that we need to lie out our life's plan by the time we are 12. If we fail to do so, we are deemed lazy or not a visionary. Even worse, if we find ourselves dissatisfied with what we have chosen or what others have chosen for us, we are viewed as being aimless or "slackers" instead of merely seeking a career or educational path that will make us happy. Being guilty of this mentality myself, I found myself falling into being judgmental when some of my own nieces did not "follow in my footsteps" and obtain 4-year degrees from colleges. I would shake my head in disbelief as they made career and educational choices that made no sense to me. However, even though I still do not understand some of the career choices they have made, I had to grudgingly acknowledge a few key things:

- They were doing things they wanted to do
- They were taking care of themselves financially
- It was not illegal

We, as women, must begin to permit ourselves flexibility in thought as it relates to our career and educational choices in order to decrease the stress such choices can cause. We must begin to recognize that the choices we make do not have to be permanent if we do not want them to be. In today's society, we have the option to change career and educational paths if we choose to do so. The age of being with the same company from graduation to retirement is no longer the standard. We are now allowed to change companies, change positions, and even change careers.

In a previous chapter, we discussed how "change can be a good thing". If we note that our current career is stressing us and when we do a cost/benefit analysis (what is good about what we do vs. what is stressing us) and the career or educational plan comes up short, we have the choice to explore other options. However, that is not to say that going down another path will be easy or can occur right away, but knowing that we can move toward a new goal can decrease the stress we are feeling at that moment in time.

Moving toward being stress-free

No one that I know is stress-free. As women, we sometimes view stress as a sign of weakness. So instead of owning up to the fact that we are stressed out, we act as if we are managing when we are truly overwhelmed. We must begin to acknowledge our stress and what causes it in order to move towards a less stressful existence. Being human and often being women, we feel the need to be the caretakers and fixers, so even if we do not have our own stress, we will often absorb that of others. We are the ones that others come "to vent" their frustration, have a shoulder to cry on, or just to assist with a solution. The goal is to recognize when things are becoming too stressful and intervene before they can cause us emotional or physical pain. A good way to do this is by preparing the antidote to stress and having it at the ready. Similar to having a First Aid kit for physical injuries, we must arm ourselves with an arsenal of healthy ways to manage stress so that we are not overwhelmed when stress happens. Just like physical injuries, stress cannot and should not be ignored. Ignoring it will only result in further and deeper injury to our emotional or physical health. Using strategies that are not healthy can also serve as a contributing factor rather than decreasing our stress.

In discussions with girlfriends, I asked them what they do to relieve stress that they find helpful. I also asked them what signs they look for to let them know it is time to bring out the Stress-Free Kit. Here are what several women reported were the ways they recognize that they are stressed and what they have in their Stress-Free Kit.

I always know that I'm stressing when I start to get back pains. It seems that my stress goes directly to my back. Depending on the level of stress the pain can either be slight or severe. I cope with stress from the spiritual perspective. I move away from being self-reliant and move toward being God- reliant. I find that it's healthy to pray and ask for help with whatever the stressor is in my life. The quicker I turn it over to Him, the quicker I get relief from the back pains and from the problem. Sometimes it takes a while because I tend to turn it over and then take it back, depending on how much control I think I have. But when I finally surrender, I get the help I need.

Surrendering moves me in the direction of finding the solutions for whatever is going on. God is not always going to fix everything the way I want it but I have faith that whatever the outcome I can deal with it. ——Danielle, 40-something

I don't deal well with stress, so I do my best not to allow it to enter my realm... I alternate between fight and flight... I realize I'm fleeing, when my house turns into a big mess and all I do is cook and eat.... I'm fighting when I get a bit cranky (or down right mean) and then a calming serenity comes over me, because I remember Who/Where I'm supposed to take all situations.... That's when my prayer life gets more centered —-Hillary, 24

As we know everyone deals with stress differently, and even some things (normal life events) cause some degree of stress such as being late for work, family life or the like. I consider myself to be pretty even-tempered and really do not allow too many things to bother me, especially things I know that I can't control.

However, when I am faced with issues and I know that I am beginning to stress, I began to lose focus and start to feel overwhelmed by things that would normally not ruffle my feathers.

Sometimes, depending on the level of what I am stressing about, I will become irritated, impatient, angry, and short with people close to me, over-analyze the situation; and if it is something of a serious nature, I have even lost sleep.

But over the years as I have matured, I have learned to look at things differently on this ride we call life. When presented with issues: we are either going to do 1 of 2 things. We will either fall apart; or deal with it in a healthy way to the best of our ability.

To cope, I have learned to do the following:

***First**- PRAY and try to be optimistic about the situation. This allows me to be grounded and focused on what I need to do, if anything. I truly believe that sometimes we cause self-inflicted stress by decisions we make or the opposite, decisions we do not make.*

As humans, we all make mistakes, but so often we do not listen to gut instinct and, ultimately, make poor decisions.

Second - I take a step back and evaluate the situation and look at the things I can control and attempt to fix them if I can. If I can't, then I simply tell myself it is what it is and this too shall pass. If I need to give myself a certain timeframe to allow myself to deal with certain feelings that I am experiencing (i.e.; anger, sadness, tension) I will do that, but after that date I just begin focusing on the issue, step by step.

Third - Sometimes we just need to reach out to others to vent or just need a shoulder to lean on or do something to take our minds off of things. So I will go dancing, or attempt to exercise.

Fourth - If it is something really bad, that is causing major chaos, then if possible, I just make the decision to eliminate it, especially negativity.

We've all made bad choices, decisions, etc., and life is much too short to continually worry about everything. Be it as it may, we have to put our best foot forward, and smile even if we don't always want to and learn to accept the things that we can't always fix or change. —Vanessa, 38

I know when I am feeling stressed, When I get the SUPERWOMAN complex. I have a need to do it all, with no help. I can do it, I know I can! Then I play some music and just sit. I go to the bedroom, turn on "Law and Order" with some snacks and chill. I have to remember to relax, which can be hard. After an evening of falling asleep without making plans, then I can be more productive—Marissa, 35

In examining the way we choose to cope, we can divide them into two coping styles—**Healthy** and **Unhealthy**.

Healthy coping involves the use of tools or strategies that decrease the experience of the current stressor, while not resulting in additional problems or stress.

Overall examples of healthy coping include:

- *Exercise*—there is a definite mind-body connection. As Danielle mentioned, the body may begin to ache or we may just stop taking care of it or abuse it when we are stressed. Exercise is a great way to address the body's needs while also allowing an outlet for pent-up emotions.
- *Music*—depending upon one's goal for decreasing stress, music can serve as the rallying cry that gets you pumped up and allows you to get out all of the frustration/anger that may be stressing you. It may also be used to soothe the soul. Determining what you want from the music will guide you in your selection—whether it is heavy metal or hardcore rap for getting out frustration, or jazz/blues to calm you.
- *Meditation*—moments of self-introspection can lead to emotional calm and peace. Meditation can come in the form of traditional chants or in simply sitting in a quiet room with your eyes closed while deep breathing.
- *Religion*-Many women with whom I talked reported that they turned to their faith to get them through difficult times.

Too Blessed to Be Stressed

Whether reading their religious text, praying, or seeking consultation with religious leaders or other people within one's faith, many women whom I have encountered discussed religion as being a major stress-reliever.

– *Other Supports*-Outside of religious supports, we sometimes lean on others around us who will offer a shoulder or a sympathetic ear. Sometimes, we want advice, but more often than not, the chance to "vent" everything that is going on to someone we can trust to keep our ranting in their confidence can be a healthy emotional outlet.

Unhealthy strategies are those that may relieve stress for a brief period of time and/or may make us at least forget it, but are likely to cause us additional problems. Examples of unhealthy coping include:

– *Internalizing*-When something is stressing us out, we may have the tendency to beat ourselves up about it. This does not mean that we should not take a realistic self-inventory of what we can do to help the situation. However, if we are placing the blame on ourselves for every wrong thing that happens in the world, or being overly critical of ourselves, that is a problem.

– *Substance Abuse*-Sometimes, when we are stressed, we just want to forget. An easy way to do so is through the use of drugs and alcohol. However, if you find that you need more than that glass of wine to unwind, or you have to reach for that cigarette, marijuana, or other substance to be able to even make it through the day, you are on a dangerous road to adding new problems versus solving the old ones.

–   *Over-eating or Not eating-* When food becomes the way in which we seek to relieve stress, we often find that it does just the opposite. We feel sluggish or even guilty about the weight we are gaining. The excess weight will often make us feel less attractive and more stressed. Yet, they do not call it "comfort food" for no reason. Even on some of the most popular television shows, it was nothing to find women commiserating over bowls of ice cream, cheesecake, or going out to dinner to address their woes. We will bury our stress in that red velvet cake or macaroni and cheese without a second thought. Yet, doing so only causes more problems.

–   *Blaming-*Instead of facing up to our own culpability in the choices we make, we instead may choose to blame others or our circumstances. When we do this, it will often evoke a feeling of helplessness that only serves to increase our stress. How many of us know of someone, or ourselves, who will grumble about not being able to live up to their potential or not having potential because they were of a certain ethnicity, social class, raised by a single parent, or (you fill in the blank)? True, we do not choose the families into which we are born, the skin that we are in, etc.—-but what we do with our life circumstances is a choice we have to make. We can choose to see the beauty in our color, look at our poverty as something to overcome and make us stronger, or we can wallow in self-pity. There is a reason why it is called wallowing—because it involves the process of drowning. We can let life circumstances suck us in to the point where we cannot emotionally breathe and feel as if we cannot keep our heads above water, or we can choose to see things in a different life with the understanding that the adversities that come our way can only make us stronger and better able to manage any stress life puts in our path.

According to Dena Patrice, an Atlanta-based personal life coach, we must begin to incorporate inner peace if we are to live a "stress-less" life. Ms. Patrice asserts that Inner peace is something that you experience at a deep level. It's when time and space no longer exist. You are present to what is happening and there are words such as "bliss & happiness" that describe it. I feel it when I am watching children sleep or laugh. It happens when I am fully expressing my authenticity (some call it a zone).

What is inner peace? According to Wikipedia, it refers to a state of being mentally and spiritually at peace, with enough knowledge and understanding to keep oneself strong in the face of discord or stress. **Being "at peace"** is considered by many to be healthy and the opposite of being stressed or anxious. Stress occurs when you respond to an event or circumstance in a way that creates mental, emotional and physical imbalances. Your heart rate goes up, your muscles tense, and you become irritable or even depressed.

What do you do when you recognize that you are "out of balance?" Here are 5 simple questions to ask when this occurs. Feel free to use all of the questions or work with one at a time.

- *What is happening in my body?* Are my muscles tense? Is there a knot in my stomach? What is happening to my heart rate? Notice what is happening to your body. Take a deep breath and relax. Continue to take deep breaths until you start to feel your muscles relax and your heart rate decrease.
- *How do I feel?* Am I angry, sad or frustrated? What am I feeling right now? Identify the emotion. Give the emotion a shape or color and simply imagine that you are looking at it. It's on the outside of you, just passing by, it's not the real you. Watch the color or shape move further and further away from you until you feel calm.
- *What thoughts am I having?* What am I telling myself? Are you saying things like…"this is too much work for one person to handle" or "how did I get myself into this situation again?" Allow all of your thoughts to come up. Let them out on paper by writing them down or go to a quiet

area and simply say them. Continue until there is nothing left to write or say.

- *How can I view this situation or circumstance from another point of view?* In other words, imagine possibilities that will create balance for you. Consider as many possibilities that you can. For instance, if you are feeling overwhelmed, then, consider eliciting others to assist you. If you are having trouble with identifying possibilities, then, think about the opposite of what caused you to feel stressed.
- *Am I choosing peace?* We have the power of free will, *The Ability to choose.* Look at your situation and ask yourself…"Is this worth losing my physical and mental health over?" How much importance are you placing on this event, circumstance or situation? What is really important and what do you care about? It's the moments that bring joy, happiness and peace in our lives that are important and what we should care about. Choose peace.

Just one moment of peace makes the world a better place to be. Practice peace.

Then, I looked within myself To the beauty of God's creation This thinking, breathing, rationalizing form that was me Recognizing the goddess within & worshipping her singing her praises in my everyday life remembering my obligation to make her happy & cherishing every aspect of this phenomenal being that was me & on that day I rested

The "S" Word

Usually, when we use the word "selfish", it is done with a roll of the eyes and a bite to our voices. For some reason, the term "selfish" has been deemed one of the worst things that a woman can be called. We have taken the concept of selfish and made it mean something abhorrent that we try to prove daily that we are not. So, when did a little selfishness become such a bad thing and how has our pursuit of demonstrating our selflessness become a disservice to us?

Men are often selfish. Yes, it is a generalization and everyone can name one who is not. Yet, why put up the energy to argue the point? Is it because we continue to harbor the belief that selfish=problematic, uncaring, or cold? What if we began to define selfish as something different? What if we started looking at it as putting ourselves first and making sure that we are okay?

In redefining selfishness, it is not meant to indicate that one stops being concerned about the needs of others or actively chooses to hurt them. Instead, it recognizes that we cannot truly be good for others unless we are good to ourselves. At what point in time did someone dictate that we must ignore our needs or wants in order to be defined as good women?

As we strive for what we have been told is the Holy Grail of Selflessness, we as women push our own dreams and needs to the side. We may try and convince ourselves that doing so is what we want, but on the inside we wonder "what if?" How many women do you know who talk about dropping out of school to raise their children, relocating from their family because their husband/boyfriend/partner got a better job somewhere else, or not pursuing some other dream to take care of siblings/parents/etc.? Now, I want you to think about how many men you know have done the same thing.

Our failure to take care of ourselves first can lead to detrimental consequences. According to the National Institute of Health, "Stressful life events such as trauma, loss of a loved one, a difficult relationship or any stressful situation-whether welcome or unwelcome-often occur before a depressive episode. Additional work and home responsibilities, caring for children and aging parents, abuse, and poverty also may trigger a depressive episode. Evidence suggests that women respond differently than men to these events, making them more prone to depression. In fact, research indicates that women respond in such a way that prolongs their feelings of stress moreso than men, increasing the risk for depression"

A friend reminded me of my first plane ride after the birth of my daughter Mia. My husband and I had decided to fly to Maryland to visit my mother-in-law. We over-packed everything, got on the plane and were ready to go. As on any flight, prior to take off, the flight attendant stood up and gave the "In Case of an Emergency" instructions. Having flown several times before, my usual inclination was to not listen and read a magazine. However, because I was flying for the first time with Mia, I gave the attendant my full attention and had to keep myself from taking notes like there would be an exam. When she got to the part about "put on your mask first before helping someone else", I looked at her as if she were crazy. There was no way I was not going to first put a mask on my precious cargo. However, in the attendant's explanation, I began to realize that, if I did not mask myself first, I would lose oxygen, become tired, and run the risk of not being able to help Mia. Such an example illustrates the need to be present for ourselves if we are going to be any good for anyone else.

I wonder if the reason we respond differently is because of our refusal to take the time to step away from stressors or allow ourselves to say that we just cannot be responsible for the situation? For some reason, we often feel compelled to offer assistance/to be there for others when we do not have the time or energy to do so. So, instead of focusing on our needs, we push them to the side in order to make sure that those around us are happy/content. How many times are we going to stay up late at night to finish a project for someone else, or run all over the city doing errands for someone while our home is neglected or the refrigerator is bare because we did not have time to do our own grocery shopping?

Society as a whole often makes it difficult for women to be selfish. We are often placed in roles where we are expected to put our needs aside and care for others. It is often our primary responsibility to care for our children, even though we did not make them on our own. Fathers not parenting their children are viewed with disapproval, while women not caring for their children are often viewed as having committed a horrendous crime. Even hospitals view our role as primary by their scheduling of "cute" classes like Boot Camp for Dads in which men are taught how to change diapers, care for their kids, etc.; while women are viewed as inherently being able to do such things.

Even when we look at wanting to pursue our dreams, it is often acceptable for us to put our dreams aside and focus on those of our loved ones. How many of you know of a friend, family member, or even yourself having moved to a new city for a partner's job, stopped pursuing some goal because you were viewed as needing to be the primary caretaker for your children/parents, etc.? Being put in the position of "what if" can cause resentment. We may experience more depressed feelings, regrets about our life's course, or even become irrationally angered at those in our lives who merely took what we often offered.

I remember becoming angry one day because I had worked on a project for someone. After staying up all night (way past my bedtime) to work on the project, I called them to get feedback before I continued on. The person informed me that they were busy and would look at it when they got the chance. It was then that I realized that, I had placed myself in a position where people around me would know that I would lose sleep/stress/work up to the last moment to complete their project; thus, they could wait until they were good and ready to work on it—*because I would make the time.* However, I would argue that I could not truly be mad at the person. After all, their need of getting the project done was being handled and because I had cheerfully agreed to do so, there was no reason for them to feel guilt/shame at having me complete it. In order to have a balanced life, the person chose to delegate responsibilities to trustworthy others while indulging in other tasks they may have had to put on the backburner. Who was I to get upset at their using their resources so that they could have "Me time"?

We must begin to make it acceptable to be selfish. It should be applauded when we pursue our dreams/ goals vs. being met with scorn that we did not stop and do for others. If we are true to ourselves, what we accomplish will be beneficial to those in our lives. The mantra of "if I am happy, everyone else will be happy. If I am fulfilled, then I am able to pass those blessings on to those in my life" should be practiced daily by women. We must recognize that we cannot be true examples for those in our lives or be the best for them if we have not allowed ourselves to live up to our own potential.

No one is saying that putting yourself first is easy. It is just the opposite—it can be quite hard. When one is used to putting their children, husband/partner, work, etc. first, it takes a lot of mental effort to begin to change the order and make yourself the priority.

Ask yourself, what dreams have I left unfulfilled because I put the needs of someone else first? Then question how fulfilling that dream may have made you a better mother/sister/friend/wife. I have a very good friend who is always saying, "If you like it, I love it." Looking at this statement, I recognized that she was saying that my wishes/wants are important and that if I am finding something beneficial, she is supportive and knows the value in it. Yet, as many of my sisters/female friends, I continue to struggle with the self-recognition that taking a moment for myself—being selfish for even a moment in time can make me a better person.

I have had friends tell me to get a massage, go buy an outfit, or take a book to Starbucks (my favorite place) and read over coffee. However, I will resist such suggestions as time-consuming or costly. Ironically, I will run to my daughter's gymnastics class, buy her a wardrobe full of new clothes, and read her a book—without the excuses used to dismiss my own needs.

Reciprocity of Selfishness

Relationships should be "give and take". We often enter them with the understanding that they will involve compromise—giving of one's self with the hope that the other person will do the same. Yet, in our fear of the "S" word, we don't often demand reciprocity. Instead, we will continue to do for others and become annoyed when the other person does not live up to the Reciprocity Principle. Our fear of being called the "S" word can keep us from getting our just due. We avoid reminding others of what we have sacrificed/done for them and that it is now our turn. It is okay to pull the Reciprocity Card in our journey toward selfishness. We need to practice feeling comfortable in asking for our time or our needs to be met from those who have taken from us.

Joyce is a 40-something married mother of two. She discussed having an epiphany about being selfish. Married to her college sweetheart, Joyce found herself following him all over the world during his military service. She unselfishly would pick up and move the whole family, find a job, or start a new business wherever they landed. Joyce talked about knowing that she needed to be unselfish at that time to further her husband's military and educational advancement. However, when it was time for her husband to leave the military, Joyce stepped up and announced to her husband that—she followed him all over the world, now they would settle down in a city of her choosing. In the end, Joyce was able to recognize that her years of unselfishness needed to be reciprocated and she had enough courage to ask for her turn.

Let's look what we need to do to embrace selfishness; we will call it the 9 Steps to Selfishness

- **I admit that I am valuable**—as women, we will often think that we do not deserve to be as valued in our relationships with others and will quietly step aside for them. If we first are able to acknowledge our own value, we can then begin the process of justifying selfishness
- **I acknowledge that I am powerful**—we have the ability to make this change and we need to not second guess it or the need for it
- **I am making the decision to begin the process of considering how my decisions will impact me**—we do this almost automatically for our partners, our children, our bosses, co-workers, friends—so we must agree to first ask, "How will this impact my goals, dreams, hope, future, and view of myself?"
- **I will self-assess**—look at what you are choosing to be selfish about and insure that you are healthy enough, realistic enough, and loving

of yourself enough to move forward in making decisions that are truly good for you. If you do not believe that you are deserving of love, or have an overall negative view of yourself, even your attempts at selfishness may prove to be problematic for you

- **I have developed "The List"**—Make a list of those who will be supportive in your newfound selfishness and ask that they assist you in "sticking to" thinking about yourself

- **I understand that people in my life may resent me for a time**—-if you are the one in the family who took in your parents when they could no longer care for themselves, was the one who stayed home on Valentine's Day watching your friends' kids/your nieces and nephews, etc so everyone else could go out, or were the one who would put off paying your own bills to ensure that your friends or family paid theirs—-prepare to be resented for a time when you choose to put yourself first. When you decide that your happiness and life are worth the same as others, it will require people around you to decrease their selfishness because they can no longer count on you to put their needs and wants first any longer. This may breed resentment in those who always relied on you to "pick up their slack". Just recognize that this anger towards you is okay and it is likely to be short in duration as those around you begin to recognize how much you truly sacrificed for them and they may begin to demonstrate more consideration for you. However, those who continue to bemoan your lack of looking after their needs and dismissing your own, may not be healthy for you in the first place, leading to step 7

- **In this journey, I need to be aware that I may lose some relationships or at the very least, some of my relationships will never be the same again**—and that is a good thing. If you "brought home part of or all of the bacon, fried it up, and did the majority or all of the household chores", in the pursuit of selfishness, you are likely to not agree to do this anymore. You will seek equity in your relationship, which may cause some resistance in the partner who was likely content with you doing most of the cooking; cleaning, parenting, etc. while still "holding it down"—and who can blame them? However, in finding your voice and asserting the need for more sharing of the responsibilities so that you feel comfortable pursuing other interests, your partner will likely have to do more, which will change the dynamics of your relationship.

- **I am willing to program my mind to ask, "How will this benefit me?"**—Such a statement allows us to get in the mindset of ensuring that we always take ourselves into consideration

- **I will seek out selfish role models**—find those around you who have demonstrated the beauty of selfishness. Early on, you may need to mimic their techniques—which may include not always being willing to be the shoulder that is cried on or insisting on "me" time in conversations vs. just being the good listener. Evaluate what you think is necessary for a good dose of selfishness, while leaving behind whatever you view as being over the top

Unacceptable Selfishness

Now that we have gotten to the point of accepting the need to be selfish, we must begin to practice it, first by recognizing what it is not acceptable

- **Totally ignoring or devaluing the needs of others**—no one is saying to put someone else in harm's way or ignore their needs in your pursuit of selfishness. We still have responsibilities to those that we love. However, consistently putting their needs before your own is also a problem
- **Being selfish in a way that will cause you harm in the long-run**—Yes, you may want to be selfish and decide that you will not pay the rent/mortgage this month because you deserve that gorgeous purse or need to go on that trip to Las Vegas. How about dropping out of school because we just don't feel like attending classes right now? However, such selfishness causes regret later on when we recognize that we have not looked at the Big Picture and have not ensured that our long-term needs will be met.

Taking a Selfish Day

With the unacceptable selfishness out of the way, it is time to make a pledge to ourselves to set aside at least one Totally Selfish Day every six months. The rules for this day include

- **Evaluate**—Every decision that is made needs to be evaluated for how it is going to (a) make you happier (b) keep you content (c) move you towards a goal. If it does not meet one of these, then it needs to wait foranother day

- **Grant yourself a wish**—it may be as simple as getting that massage you have been craving, indulging in a hot bath, getting a manicure, or just getting some quiet time. Whatever you have been thinking "I wish I could/had/did" today is the day to do it
- **Make it a No-Buy Day**—this means that you cannot spend money on anyone else. This is your day. As we know, we will spend our money/time on those around us, as we do without. If your child/partner/mother/father, etc. needs something, stock up on it the day before because today is the day that, if any money is spent, it is just on you
- **Live Guilt-Free**—-as an old commercial says "I am worth it"—remind yourself that you have *earned* this day. If the partner/child/parent, etc. calls you for anything less than an emergency, allow yourself to feel okay with telling them that you cannot do it that day.
- **Have your back-up team in place**—situations happen. Commitments happen. Even on Selfish Day, we cannot stop being wife/partner/mother/daughter/friend. However, we can find that person in our life who will "pick up the slack" on our day. It might be a sister-friend, mother, partner, or husband. This is anyone that you know will not begrudge you your day, but instead will do the errands, watch your children, etc. so that you can have your time without anxiety

- **Send out The Warning**—if you are the go-to person in your family or friendship circle, you owe everyone the courtesy of letting them know that this is your day. When people are used to counting on you, they will expect that Selfish Day is a day like any other. The goal is to enjoy yourself—not burn bridges or violate rule #4 when the people in your life come calling on your day.
- **Don't Share**—today is not something that you collaborate with your friends or sisters. When we do something in conjunction with others, compromise has to happen. Your friend may decide that a fun thing to do would be going to a club while you just want to curl up with a book and some Starbucks coffee. Sharing this day will inevitably result in some level of discussion and negotiation about what should occur—defeating the whole purpose of your own day. Plus, these same friends may need to be your back-up team to put out all of the small fires that occur while you are sipping that coffee and enjoying your book.
- **Do Share**—yes, it seems contradictory. However, be willing to share the beauty of the Selfish Day with your sisters and female friends. Tell them about how wonderful it can be and encourage them to take their own day at some other point in time. Selfish Day is a gift that is meant to be passed on to others.

My Selfish Day Declaration

I hereby declare that on _____,
I am going to take a Selfish Day. As a part of my
Selfish Day, I will be doing the following:
1. _____
2. _____
3. _____
4. _____

I have made sure that all of the above are going to
benefit me, be for me, and about me. The people
who will be my Back-Up on this day are
1. _____
2. _____
3. _____

I have consulted with them and they are prepared
to be there for my family, friends, etc. so that I do
not have to worry about anything interfering with
my day. I acknowledge that I deserve this day and
promise to enjoy it.

"I Am My Sister's Keeper"

"I don't have female friends"

I remember one time conducting a seminar for twenty-something college women where I encouraged them to embrace sisterhood with other women. A young lady stood up in the session and proudly declared, " I don't have any female friends." When I asked why, she bluntly told me "because they are catty." Shaking my head, I looked at her and quietly stated, "but *you* are a woman." It amazes me at times how we, as women, will quickly point out the negatives about each other. Let's do an experiment. I want you to think about all of the negative attributes you have placed on women in the past. To make it easier for you, I will start it out by listing the ones I have heard.

Women are:
- catty
- backstabbers
- sneaky
- not trustworthy

Don't be shy. Add to the list—you know that you have more. They may be characteristics that you mumbled under your breath or ones you have proudly declared to the masses (like the young lady in my seminar). It is amazing that we do not see the irony in our negative characterizations of women. Even in developing the title of this book, I was in places with female mental health providers who shook their heads and stated they would not work with girls because "girls got issues." Yet, every one of us in the room were girls at one point in time, and it was usually other women (our mothers, grandmothers, aunts, etc.) who were there to guide us. At what point will we as women begin to give each other "the benefit of the doubt"? How about getting to the point when we acknowledge the role we need to play in each other's lives instead of quickly dismissing the importance of sisterhood?

Have any of you noticed the popularity of advice columns and books written by men about the experiences of women? Many of them have been bestsellers as we rush to purchase books that tell us what we need to do to: (1) get or keep a man, (2) love ourselves, or (3) achieve our goals. We seem to be open to embracing the advice of men to tell us about ourselves, but will mumble, roll our eyes, or tune-out when other women stand in our faces and offer us the same advice. Logic would suggest that we would be more open to advice from others who may have experienced the same thing, but instead, we dismiss them and call them the names we listed above. At some point, we must move beyond the belief that women are "messy," "catty," or any other terms we choose to use. If our perception includes such beliefs, we will look for signs that they are true. We will judge our fellow women with a misplaced comment or action instead of recognizing it as a mere mistake.

I remember a time when I had gotten off on the wrong foot with a female at a past job. Being a person who often has several projects going at the same time, I have a tendency to forget niceties and come into a room like a tornado, rattle off whatever I need to ensure that others know, and then go back to the projects that I am juggling. During my first interaction with this new female co-worker, she viewed my behavior as rude and used it to justify future negative interactions with me. However, I wonder if the reaction would have been different if I had not been a woman? Would the first leap have been to perceive that I was rude, disrespectful, or that I looked down on her; or would she have looked for some other, less negative explanation for my behavior? Not at any point in time am I claiming that my behavior followed the rules of genteel society, but did it qualify for future ill treatment and unwillingness to even pursue a collegial relationship?

Reality check—how many of us have put our x-ray eyes on to another woman when she enters the workplace or when she tries to join our social circle, etc? Have you tried to find the chinks in her armor or focused instead on the pieces that are shiny and put together? Better yet, did you notice the chinks and resolve to help repair them? There was a movie by Spike Lee in which the character was asked, "Are you your brother's keeper?" to which the young man yelled with enthusiasm, "Yes, I am!" How many of us can truly say that we are our sister's keeper? Can we say that our mission in life is to embrace other women and be supportive forces for each other? Even when we say it, how have our actions gone totally against the concept?

Diana is a 50-something married mother of one. After the death of her mother when she was in her early 20s, Diana's father chose to marry his mistress. Diana's relationship with her now-stepmother has always been filled with a high level of animosity. When asked about the conflict with her stepmother, Diana likes to point out how she does not like the woman because she had been her father's mistress. Many would understand Diana's point and likely feel the same way. Yet, ironically, Diana continued to have an excellent relationship with her father, whom she does not seem to hold accountable for the affair. Such a discrepancy is interesting in that the mistress, now stepmother, was not friends with the mother. Therefore, she did not technically owe Diana's mother anything. Yet, Diana did not hold her father accountable for being the one to violate the marital vow.

Another example is that of Leslie, 23 whom I met during a women's group. Leslie openly told the other members of the group how she was going to fight another woman because the woman had dared to sleep with Leslie's man. When I asked Leslie how she was doing now that she and her man had broken up, she looked at me like I was crazy and informed me that she and her boyfriend were still together.

A last example that was in the media around the time of writing the first draft of this book was the story of a famous couple in which the husband was found to have been unfaithful. Rumors had swirled around that the husband had been cheating, which he denied. However, soon the husband admitted to his affair. The Wife then came out blasting the Other Woman for being a home wrecker. Initially, like many women, I quickly aligned myself with The Wife who was battling another woman "seducing" her husband. However, as The Wife continued to berate The Other Woman while remaining at the side of her husband, my own indignation at The Other Woman diminished and became uncomfortable to me. Sure, the language was nicer, but the situation was beginning to play out like the one in my women's group. Much later, The Other Woman had her own say and began to blast The Wife back, calling her names that implied that she [The Wife] was overbearing. In the next breath, The Other Woman went on to lament how much the unfaithful husband had been through and how she still loved him. Again, not saying that either of the women should have befriended the other, but instead of focusing their energies on the common denominator, they chose instead to blame The Other Woman for the problems in their love lives. I can only speculate how things may have been different if, in solidarity and sisterhood, The Other Woman had, instead of beginning a relationship with Mr. Unfaithful, rebuffed him and informed The Wife of his advances. Not saying that The Wife would have been open to it, but if we as women began to "have each other's back", there would be a lot less room for someone to pit us against each other for their own benefit.

How many of us have loudly described another woman using negative terms, have threatened to fight or fought someone over someone we were dating because they dared to violate the Sacred Sisterhood? Yet, at the same time, we clearly let the man in our life know that we did not value the sisterhood, either because we were willing to forgive him, let him continue to share our bed, have children by him, or otherwise show a long-term commitment in spite of the fact that he betrayed our trust? We make it clear that we assume that there is something wrong with the sister versus recognizing that it is the person whom we are dating that has the problem. Having brothers, I have seen them shrug when someone they are dating cheats and they quickly choose to leave them. They do not fight the other guy, threaten him, or engage in any of the other behavior because they have placed the blame squarely where it belongs— on the shoulder of the person with whom they had the commitment. Sometimes, we wonder why males do not seem to have as much drama. Can it be, in part, due to the fact that they value the brotherhood bond and are willing to give each other the benefit of the doubt?

Looking at it the other way, how many of us have been on the other end? How many of us have listened as he has complained about his wife/mother of his kids/ live-in girlfriend, etc. and we justify our relationship with him by saying she is not fulfilling her role? How many of us have seen how he treats the mother of his children/wife/ex-wife and clap with glee at his disrespect and say that it is acceptable because she must have done something wrong to deserve it? In our actions, we again show that we do not respect the Sisterhood of Women. We have shown him that it is acceptable to treat another woman in a disrespectful manner. Then, we are surprised when we become the wife/ex-wife/ mother of his children/live-in girlfriend and we receive the same level of disrespect.

Can you think of a woman who, in your first interaction, you quickly dismissed her as messy, crazy, etc., but then recognized that your first impression was an inaccurate one? How would the sisterhood of women be more powerful if we forced ourselves to begin identifying the positives in other women before we begin looking at the negative? Many will say that such a task is impossible, because women are

Catty
Messy
Drama Queens

However, as we each are women, if we first engaged in some self-examination and made sure that, on an individual basis, we were not

Catty
Messy
Drama Queens

We would have examples of one less woman who falls into that stereotype.

Having been in administrative roles, I have seen firsthand the failure to be supportive of each other. How many of us have gone into a new job, been embraced by the men with whom we work while clearly being sized up by the women in the office? On the other side, how many of us have been the one doing the sizing up? At some point, we as women have remained in the era before Women's Liberation when we were counted as a quota within businesses. We still seem to believe, in spite of statistics indicating that we are more than half of the workforce, that there is only room for one of us in the office. Instead of viewing each other as supports, we instead will view each other as competition. Such a mindset automatically impacts how we treat each other. Instead of showing each other the ropes, we try to hang each other with it. We refuse to share our knowledge about the working of the company, the best ways to get tasks accomplished, or to offer any other assistance.

So, how do we get beyond the spirit of competition and instead move towards *Embracing the Sisterhood?*

Embracing the Sisterhood

First, we must realize that, we as women *are in this together.* We are the ones who choose to place ourselves in competition with each other. As women, we may share similar experiences and goals. Yet, instead of leaning on each other for support and recognizing how powerful we can be if we band together, we choose to engage in in-fighting. At some point, we must begin to recognize what the movie industry, food industry, and clothing industries have noticed— women can be a driving force when they choose to use their Strength In Numbers.

Second, we must be willing to *allow failure to be an option* and if, *at first we don't succeed, we need to try again.* It is amazing how many women will report that they do not have female friends because of one female friend who stabbed them in the back, let them down, etc. We are so quick to give up on all women for the mistake of one. Yet, at the same time, there are many of us who can point to a man in our lives who hurt our feelings, cheated on us, or otherwise let us down, but did not keep us from continuing to pursue a dating or marital relationship with another man. Sometimes, one must fail in a sister-friendship in order to really appreciate a good one, or just to figure out what they do not want in a sister-friend.

Third, we must *engage in self-evaluation*. By self-evaluation, we must be willing to actively take a critical look at ourselves. In doing so, we recognize the good, bad, and the ugly that we are "putting out there" and actively examine ways to be better people. We must ensure that we embody the traits that other women would want in a sister-friend. It might not be that there are not any good sister-friends out there, it may be your own presence that is keeping the good ones from wanting you within their circle. We must make sure that we are not the overly competitive one, the backstabber, or the Drama Queen before we can find sister-friends who are good for us.

Activity-Am I Ready to Be My Sister's Keeper?

This activity is in three parts.

Part 1: Write down a list of characteristics that make you a great sister-friend. Don't be modest. Make sure that you include everything. Remember, this is just for you to see.

> Part 2: Now, this gets a little harder and requires a willingness to be brutally honest with yourself. Write down those things about yourself that make you not the greatest person to be around.
>
> Part 3: List the characteristics of sister-friends you require. Compare them to your own two lists. Do you find that you embody the characteristics that you demand of others? Do you notice that some of the things that are problematic about yourself are also ones that you refuse to accept in others? We must be willing to have realistic expectations for those around us if we are to make our female friendships work.

Now that we know what needs to happen before we can be open to being Our Sisters' Keeper, how do we begin to foster such relationships?

- **Find a group in existence**—I was fortunate to become a member of a sorority in college. Such an experience provided me with a ready-made group of sister-friends whom I have continued to love throughout my life. However, sororities are not for everyone, but there are other groups that are available. My sister-in-law has joined a book club, others have volunteered with community non-profit agencies, or found other groups already in existence that have permitted them the opportunity to find like-minded women with whom to begin friendships

- **Walk down memory lane**—in the age of Facebook, MySpace, and Google, it is easier to find those with whom we had connections in childhood. If you had a female friend that you remember with fondness, maybe this is the sister-friend with whom to re-connect
- **Treat them like men**—many of us have been hurt in intimate relationships. Yet, we continue to pursue love with men. Instead of giving up on all men, we try to "learn lessons" from the relationship and move on. We need to begin to give other women the same courtesy

---

A Pledge to My Sisters
Recognizing that there is Strength In Numbers, I resolve to be there for my sisters. My sisters are not just related to me by blood, but by common goals, faith, love, and trust. I will strive to make and maintain contact with my sisters for it is through their support and love that I become a better woman.

Reflections On My "Issues"

From this book, I have learned the following about myself and my issues

_____

_____

_____

_____

_____

_____

_____

_____

_____

_____

_____

_____

In learning more about myself, I realize that I have valuable lessons to share with my sister-friends so that they, too can work on their issues and learn from them. Below is the wisdom that I need to pass on to my daughters, nieces, and sister-friends so that they face less issues.

_____

_____

_____

_____

_____

_____

_____

_____

_____

Portions of the profits from online retailer
sales of this book will be donated to First Purse, Inc.
First Purse, Inc. is an innovative nonprofit organization
that empowers girls, ages 8 to 10, to be financially
literate, invest in their communities and to own their
"first purse" of financial independence.

To find out more about First Purse, Inc. please visit the
organization's website at www.firstpurse.org

About the Author

Dr. Tyffani Monford Dent is a licensed psychologist. She is a lecturer, trainer, and consultant on topics related to working with children and adolescents as well as women's issues. Dr. Dent is the Clinical Coordinator at a residential treatment center as well as being in private practice. She is the loving wife of Travis and the proud mother of two future "women"— Mia & Zoe.

Dr. Dent can be reached
Via email at:
drtyff@yahoo.com
Or on the web:
www.monforddentconsulting.com

7694999R0

Made in the USA
Charleston, SC
01 April 2011